Whitehall...

The Permanent Crisis
Iran's Nuclear Trajectory

Shashank Joshi

www.rusi.org

Royal United Services Institute for Defence and Security Studies

The Permanent Crisis: Iran's Nuclear Trajectory
Shashank Joshi
First published 2012

Whitehall Papers series

Series Editor: Professor Malcolm Chalmers
Editors: Adrian Johnson and Ashlee Godwin

RUSI is a Registered Charity (No. 210639)
ISBN 978-0-415-83256-4

Published on behalf of the Royal United Services Institute for Defence
and Security Studies
by
Routledge Journals, an imprint of Taylor & Francis, 4 Park Square,
Milton Park, Abingdon OX14 4RN

SUBSCRIPTIONS
Please send subscription orders to:

USA/Canada: Taylor & Francis Inc., Journals Department, 325 Chestnut Street,
8th Floor, Philadelphia, PA 19106, USA

UK/Rest of World: Routledge Journals, T&F Customer Services, T&F Informa UK Ltd,
Sheepen Place, Colchester, Essex CO3 3LP, UK

Contents

About the Author

Shashank Joshi is a Research Fellow at RUSI and a doctoral student of international relations at Harvard University's Department of Government. He specialises in the international security of South Asia and the Middle East. He has published peer-reviewed work in academic journals, commented on international affairs for radio and television, and is a regular contributor to newspapers including the *New York Times*, *Financial Times*, *Daily Telegraph*, *Guardian*, *Hindu* and *Times of India*.

Shashank holds Master's degrees from Cambridge and Harvard, and previously graduated with a Starred First in politics and economics from Gonville and Caius College, Cambridge University. During 2007–08, he was a Kennedy Scholar from Britain to the United States.

He has taught as a supervisor and teaching fellow at both Cambridge and Harvard. He has also worked for the National Democratic Institute in Moscow on electoral analysis and democratic training projects, Citigroup in New York in their regulatory reporting division, and in RUSI's Asia Programme on India and global security issues. He is a graduate of the Columbia-Cornell Summer Workshop on the Analysis of Military Operations and Strategy.

His recent publications include 'India's Military Instrument: A Doctrine Stillborn', *Journal of Strategic Studies* (forthcoming, 2013); 'Transition from Assad', in 'Syria Crisis Briefing: A Collision Course for Intervention', RUSI Briefing Paper, 25 July 2012; 'China-India Relations: Awkward Ascents', *Orbis* (Fall 2011); 'Reflections on the Arab Revolutions: Order, Democracy, and Western Policy', *RUSI Journal* (Vol. 156, No. 2, April 2011); 'China, India and the "Whole Set-Up and Balance of the World"', *STAIR: St. Antony's International Review* (Vol. 6, No. 2, February 2011); and 'India's AfPak Strategy', *RUSI Journal* (Vol. 155, No. 1, March 2010).

Acknowledgements

I am extremely grateful to all those who supported me in the writing of this Whitehall Paper. Malcolm Chalmers was exceptionally generous with his time and expertise. He offered extensive guidance from start to finish, and carefully read several drafts of the manuscript. Andrea Berger and Hugh Chalmers were similarly helpful, and I could not have done without their frequent advice, particularly on a great number of technical issues. The paper benefited from the patient and expert editing of Adrian Johnson, with Ashlee Godwin. Saqeb Mueen and Daniel Sherman have been unfailingly supportive colleagues.

Many other individuals provided feedback, whether in writing or in conversation. Some of these would wish to remain anonymous, but I particularly want to thank Ali Ansari, Nick Beadle, Julian Borger, Jonathan Eyal, Peter Jenkins, Frank O'Donnell, Andreas Persbo, Ian Stewart, Sir Harold Walker, and Heather Williams. I am grateful to others who commented on drafts at two workshops held at RUSI in June and August 2012. Finally, my greatest debt of gratitude is to Hannah Cheetham, Sundanda Joshi and Vinit Joshi.

Any remaining errors or shortcomings are, of course, mine alone.

Acronyms and Abbreviations

CBI	Central Bank of Iran
CIA	Central Intelligence Agency
GCC	Gulf Cooperation Council
HEU	Highly enriched uranium
IAEA	International Atomic Energy Agency
IDF	Israeli Defense Forces
ILSA	Iran and Libya Sanctions Act
IRGC	Iranian Revolutionary Guards Corps
LEU	Low-enriched uranium
MEU	Medium-enriched uranium
NATO	North Atlantic Treaty Organization
NIE	National Intelligence Estimate
NPT	Nuclear Non-Proliferation Treaty
OPEC	Organization of Petroleum Exporting Countries
RUSI	Royal United Services Institute
SIPRI	Stockholm International Peace Research Institute
SIS	Secret Intelligence Service
TRR	Tehran Research Reactor
UAE	United Arab Emirates
UK	United Kingdom
UN	United Nations
US	United States
USSR	Union of Soviet Socialist Republics

Map

Map 1: Approximate ranges of Iranian ballistic-missile systems.

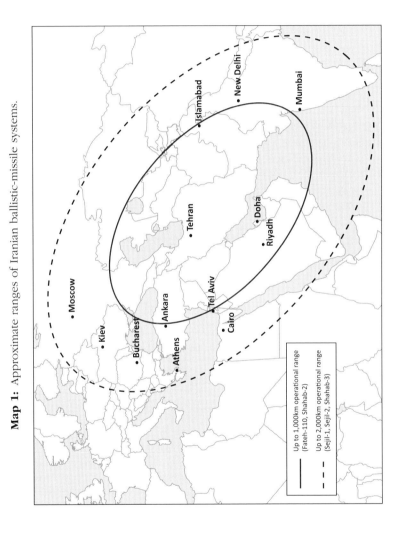

Up to 1,000km operational range
(Fateh-110, Shahab-2)

Up to 2,000km operational range
(Sejil-1, Sejil-2, Shahab-3)

I. INTRODUCTION

Six years ago, in mid-2006, Iran had no centrifuges spinning and possessed no enriched uranium. Robert Joseph, the US under secretary of state for arms control, declared that year: 'we cannot have a single centrifuge spinning in Iran. Iran is a direct threat to the national security of the United States and our allies'.[1]

Today, as President Barack Obama prepares to begin his second term, Iran has installed over 9,000 centrifuges, and has produced 6,876 kg of uranium enriched to 3.5 per cent, known as low-enriched uranium (LEU).[2] By the end of 2012, Iran could easily have enriched enough uranium to 20 per cent (still LEU, but described here as medium-enriched uranium, or 'MEU', for clarity) to suffice for one nuclear bomb, if that were enriched further to weapons-grade. Iran instead chose to convert much of its MEU stockpile into reactor fuel, but it is not clear whether it will continue to do so.[3]

The quickening pace of Iran's nuclear activities, and its growing degree of 'nuclear latency' – a state's temporal and technical proximity to acquiring a usable nuclear device – has produced a sense of urgency amongst a number of countries, including Arab rivals of Iran. Iran's dogged pursuit of nuclear technology in the face of unprecedented pressure has also placed new stresses on the Iranian state itself. Indeed, a former senior Iranian diplomat, Seyed Hossein Mousavian, observes in his recently released memoirs that 'the nuclear crisis has been the most important challenge facing the Islamic Republic's foreign policy apparatus since the 1980–88 war between Iran and Iraq'.[4]

---

[1] Seymour M Hersh, 'The Iran Plans: Would President Bush Go to War to Stop Tehran from Getting the Bomb?', *New Yorker*, 17 April 2006.

[2] International Atomic Energy Agency (IAEA), 'Implementation of the NPT Safeguards Agreement and Relevant Provisions of Security Council Resolutions in the Islamic Republic of Iran', GOV/2012/37, 30 August 2012, p. 3.

[3] LEU ordinarily refers to any uranium enriched below the level of 20 per cent, and HEU (highly enriched uranium) to any uranium enriched to a greater degree. Here, the term MEU (medium-enriched uranium) is used to denote uranium enriched to that boundary level, so as to capture an important difference between this and lower-grade quantities.

[4] Seyed Hossein Mousavian, *The Iranian Nuclear Crisis: A Memoir* (Washington, DC: Carnegie Endowment for International Peace, 2012), p. 1.

The first quarter of 2012 was especially fraught. Fears of an Israeli military attack on Iranian nuclear facilities peaked, European and American sanctions on Iran intensified, and Iran enriched uranium at its fastest-ever pace. A round of talks during 2012, beginning in April in Istanbul and concluding in June in Moscow, briefly eased this tension. However, these negotiations have failed, with Iran expecting but being refused sanctions relief, and the West remaining dissatisfied with Iran's continued enrichment and lack of co-operation with the International Atomic Energy Agency (IAEA). The dialogue has now been downgraded to expert-level rather than political-level, reflecting the dim prospects of a settlement. Although the domestic political flux in the United States has now eased, making it easier for the second Obama administration to demonstrate flexibility in nuclear talks, Iran's own politics are not going to stabilise until at least June 2013, when President Mahmoud Ahmadinejad will be replaced. This means that, despite the encouraging prospect of direct US-Iran talks beginning as early as November or December 2012, diplomacy might still struggle to find traction over the short-term, as sanctions begin to bite deeply.

In the interim, Iran's growing stockpile of enriched uranium, some of it enriched almost to the point of weapons-grade quality, casts a shadow over this process. With every passing month, Iran is perceived to have shortened the time it requires to acquire nuclear weapons, should it choose and attempt to do so. Chapter II explores how far Iran stands from a nuclear weapon in technical terms, whether it wants nuclear weapons at all, and how the US and Iran, as well as other participants in this crisis, might come to an agreement that addresses each of their concerns.

While it would be extremely difficult for Iran to successfully dash for nuclear weapons without being detected and subsequently attacked, this does not mean that it is impossible for it to do so. Moreover, as outlined in greater detail in Chapter III, any military action, particularly if undertaken unilaterally by Israel, would probably cause a delay of only two to three years to Iran's nuclear programme, and would have the adverse effect of pushing it further underground and further out of the sight of international inspectors and spies. Although one might say that the Iranian nuclear crisis began in 2002, with the public revelation of undeclared nuclear sites, many of the last decade's concerns date to the very beginning of Iran's nuclear programme in the era of the Shah. Yet, despite the present state of elevated tensions, the stand-off might very well stretch on for years without settlement. Even war is more likely to produce a metastasised crisis than resolution. In a very real sense, therefore, we are already in a seemingly 'permanent crisis', one that has lasted far longer than the short, sharp confrontations that characterise international politics.

Objectives

The purpose of this study is threefold. The first objective is to situate Iran's nuclear programme in the context of the security concerns of all of the interested parties, including Iran itself. The nuclear dispute is embedded in a set of overlapping security disputes between Iran on the one hand and the United States, Arab regional powers, Israel and the broader 'West' on the other. Even within the umbrella group for nuclear talks with Iran – the six states (the US, UK, France, China, Russia and Germany) known collectively as the P5 + 1 – individual members have different strategic or ideological rationales for engaging with or putting pressure on Iran; different thresholds for what would constitute a nuclear-weapons-capable Iran; and different levels of antipathy to Iran's broader foreign policy. Chapter II of this study examines how Iran's nuclear programme, which enjoyed widespread international support in the 1960s and 1970s, became the most scrutinised nuclear programme in history, subject to unprecedented interference and sabotage. This section also explores Iran's changing position within broader regional and global security issues, structures and alignments.

The present level of Iranian-Israeli antagonism is fairly recent, with the two states having co-operated extensively in the 1970s and 1980s, in part out of mutual fear of Saddam Hussein's revisionist Iraq.[5] The policies of European states towards Iran have also evolved over the past decades. Some European states resisted American calls to put pressure on Iran in the 1990s, but it is also European states – France and the UK, in particular – that have been the most enthusiastic about its application over the past six years. In other words, diplomatic alignments and even interpretations of national interests have proven flexible.

Moreover, some of the obstacles to a settlement of the *nuclear* issue – including Iranian distrust over the reliability of international guarantees and American scepticism over engaging with Iran on non-nuclear security issues – have their genesis in older, *security*-related aspects of the interaction between the interested parties. Iran's own threat perceptions in the face of changes in the Middle East, from the unrest in Syria to the possible re-establishment of Iraq as an Arab power, to the rise of Turkish influence, will affect Tehran's calculus regarding the option of building nuclear weapons. A coda to Chapter II examines how the Arab Spring has affected Iranian security and how, for instance, the fall of the Assad regime in Syria might affect Iran's position in nuclear talks.

The second objective is to situate this examination of Iran in a comparative and thematic context. A large volume of information is available on, for instance, the historic efficacy of economic sanctions; on

---

[5] Trita Parsi, *Treacherous Alliance: The Secret Dealings of Israel, Iran, and the U.S.* (New Haven: Yale University Press, 2007), ch. 2.

the influences that weigh upon states when deciding whether to pursue nuclear weapons; and on the ways in which states can and cannot use nuclear weapons as instruments of coercion or aggression.

Too often, Iran is seen to be *sui generis*. In fact, the experience of Iraq in the 1990s or South Africa in the 1980s can help to inform an assessment of how Iran will be affected by, and respond to, intense multilateral economic and political pressure. The experience of Iraq in the 1980s and early 1990s can improve understanding of how Iran's bureaucratic arrangements and management of the nuclear programme will constrain the pace at which it develops. The experience of emerging and former nuclear powers, like India, Pakistan and South Africa, can provide indications as to how a nuclear Iran might define its nuclear posture and doctrine. These are imperfect comparisons but, given the opacity of the Iranian political system and speculative nature of these questions, such precedents are nonetheless useful. Chapter IV, which looks at the implications of a nuclear Iran, asks whether and how Pakistan's experience in using nuclear weapons might be usefully applied to Iran.

The third objective is to consider how policy responses by the West will and should evolve were Iran to resume its alleged nuclear-weapons programme, continue to undertake some degree of near-weaponisation or weaponisation,[6] or test and deploy nuclear weapons.

Current efforts to consider this question publicly run into two types of problems. The first is that, as James Dobbins and his co-authors observe, 'Western policymakers shy away from addressing this prospect, lest they seem to be acquiescing to something they deem unacceptable and want to prevent'.[7] President Obama declared in March 2012 that 'Iran's leaders should understand that I do not have a policy of containment; I have a policy to prevent Iran from obtaining a nuclear weapon'.[8] This was a rhetorical flourish rather than a nuanced statement of policy, but it highlights the cognitive – and political – challenges of thinking through and articulating a Plan B, lest prevention fail.

Indeed, there are multiple definitions of failure, in this context. Iran could stop just short of weaponisation, thereby remaining below President Obama's articulated threshold, and *still* exhibit behaviours thought to be characteristic of some nuclear-armed states, such as heightened risk-acceptance and self-confidence. By some accounts, even possession of a

---

[6] In this study, the term 'weaponisation' denotes the fabrication of a usable nuclear device.

[7] James Dobbins, Alireza Nader, Dalia Dassa Kaye and Frederic Wehrey, *Coping with a Nuclearizing Iran* (Santa Monica, CA: RAND Corporation, 2011), p. ix.

[8] Barack Obama, 'Remarks by the President at AIPAC Policy Conference', The White House, 4 March 2012.

Significant Quantity[9] of fissile material would accord a country nuclear-weapon status.[10] Although this is clearly an unhelpfully low threshold – by such measures, Iran would be nuclear-armed as soon as it acquired more than approximately 380 kg of MEU – it reflects the fluidity of the concept of nuclear capability. This fluidity means that policy must be responsive and adaptable.

It is therefore imperative to lay the intellectual groundwork for policies that address the challenges of a nuclear Iran – whether this entails containment, coercion, engagement or all three – rather than assume that such an outcome (an Iranian nuclear weapon) cannot come about. Chapter IV of this Whitehall Paper argues that a nuclear Iran could take many forms, but that there would be incentives for Iran to assume a limited nuclear posture. It also contends that, regardless of what form any Iranian nuclear weapons might take, Tehran's ability to use its nuclear weapons as instruments of coercion is constrained in important ways by geography, conventional military capabilities, and the logic of nuclear strategy.

The second problem is that in some cases where authors *have* described the consequences and policy challenges of a nuclear Iran, there has been an assumption that Iranian weaponisation would spark an inevitable arms race. These assessments are part of a longstanding debate between proliferation pessimists and optimists.

Yet, it is important to understand and assess the full range of incentives and constraints faced by any would-be proliferant rather than assume a dystopian proliferation cascade. Historically, analysts have consistently over-estimated the likelihood that weaponisation by one state will cause its rivals to follow suit. This paper sets out a variety of reasons why Saudi Arabia, Turkey and Egypt might be considerably less likely to seek nuclear weapons than has been hitherto argued.

Chapter II opens by describing Iran's nuclear trajectory since the 1950s, and particularly since the nuclear crisis recognisably began, a decade ago, in August 2002. This section places these nuclear developments in the broader context of Iran's foreign and security policies, with the

---

[9] A Significant Quantity is defined by the IAEA as 'the approximate amount of nuclear material for which the possibility of manufacturing a nuclear explosive device cannot be excluded'. The present threshold for uranium is 25 kg of Uranium-235 (U-235) in HEU or 75 kg of U-235 in MEU (which would be present in roughly 380 kg of MEU). These thresholds are contested by critics, who argue that they should be revised downwards considerably. See *IAEA Safeguards Glossary: 2001 Edition*, International Nuclear Verification Series No. 3 (Vienna: International Atomic Energy Agency, 2002), p. 23.
[10] Jacques E C Hymans, 'When Does a State Become a "Nuclear Weapon State"? An Exercise in Measurement Validation', *Nonproliferation Review* (Vol. 17, No. 1, March 2010), p. 161.

intention of understanding the factors driving Iran's nuclear ambitions. Chapter II also asks how Iran has historically responded to pressure, and whether 2003 – the year when Iran is thought to have paused its nuclear-weapons programme – offers lessons in this regard.

Finally, this section asks how the Arab Spring has affected Iranian policy since 2011, and whether the collapse of the Syrian regime would alter Iran's security calculus and, by extension, its nuclear thinking.

Chapter III focuses on the current status of activity to contain or resolve the Iranian nuclear crisis. It analyses why diplomatic talks have failed; how changing political conditions in Washington and Tehran might make it easier to strike a deal; and whether the campaign of sanctions, sabotage, assassinations and cyber-warfare launched against Iran's nuclear programme has been successful. This section also looks in more detail at the military option, concluding that any strike against Iran would be deeply counterproductive, and outlines a set of principles that should shape any compromise with Iran.

Finally, Chapter IV examines a scenario in which Iran obtains nuclear weapons. While recognising that this remains highly unlikely, this section asks what factors would shape Iran's nuclear posture; how Iranian behaviour might be affected; and whether other states would respond with nuclear weapons of their own. It questions the assumptions and logic of alarmist studies – those which see a nuclear Iran as fanatical, unresponsive to deterrence and certain to precipitate a wave of unstoppable nuclear proliferation – whilst outlining the very real risks that would flow from such a failure of Western policy.

II. HOW WE GOT HERE, AND WHERE WE STAND

This section outlines Iran's nuclear trajectory, and the interaction between nuclear and security developments over time. The purpose is to better understand the factors underlying Iran's nuclear choices and the manner in which Iran responds to pressure.

Paradoxically, threats to the Iranian regime appear to induce both expansion and recession in nuclear activities at different times, suggesting a highly non-linear relationship between outside pressure and Iranian nuclear policy. It is likely that, at certain points, the application of pressure on Iran has effected changes in Iran's nuclear policy. However, there is reason to suppose that the specific nature of that pressure (the credibility of a threatened ground invasion in 2003, for example) has been crucial, and that similar pressure applied at different moments might not yield the same result and may even be counterproductive.

Moreover, domestic politics within Iran has been an essential element in determining the importance placed on the nuclear programme, and therefore the receptivity to policy changes in the face of pressure. Those factions who place a higher priority on international co-operation have, at times, been more favourable towards conciliatory policies that accept limits on the nuclear programme.

However, there is no clear relationship between political moderation and nuclear commitment. At its most avowedly revolutionary stage, just after the revolution of 1979, Iran rejected the nuclear programme. In contrast, nuclear activities, including the construction of clandestine nuclear facilities, continued during the reformist interlude, 1997–2005. Those considered by the West to be reformist leaders also rejected nuclear concessions in the negotiations of 2009, in concordance with their so-called hard-line counterparts. Notably, the reformist leader Mir Hossein Mousavi, who was amongst these rejectionists, had earlier opposed Iran's suspension of its nuclear programme in 2003 during negotiations with the EU.[1]

---

[1] Trita Parsi, *A Single Roll of the Dice: Obama's Diplomacy with Iran* (New Haven, CT: Yale University Press, 2012), Kindle edition, location 1461 (ch. 3).

Today, regime *cohesion* may be a more important factor than factional *ideology*. With rivalry between the supreme leader and President Mahmoud Ahmadinejad subsiding as a result of the latter's political decline,[2] the supreme leader may grow more amenable to compromise without fear that such a deal would either become a dangerous wedge issue, pitting Iranian factions against one another at a sensitive time, or empower Ahmadinejad, a lame duck waiting to leave office in the summer of 2013.

Iran's Nuclear Trajectory

Iran's nuclear ambitions have a long pedigree. In the 1960s and 1970s, Iran developed an ambitious and internationally sourced nuclear programme. The growth of that programme hints at the techno-nationalist and energy-generation motivations that continue to characterise at least parts of Iran's contemporary nuclear activities. At the same time, its collapse and covert renewal in the decades after 1979 laid the groundwork for some of the present distrust between Iran and its erstwhile nuclear collaborators.

From 1957 to 1979

From 1957 onwards, the United States offered extensive nuclear co-operation with then-ally Iran, which signed the Nuclear Non-Proliferation Treaty (NPT) in 1968. Over the course of this period, the US directly supplied Iran with enriched uranium and a nuclear research reactor, the Tehran Research Reactor (TRR). A broad range of countries assisted Iran during this period. Germany and France supplied reactors, while over half of Iran's energy commission personnel were thought to be Argentine, with advisers from the UK, the US and India.[3] Iran also negotiated with other states, including Belgium, China, Italy and Switzerland.[4]

Iran later agreed to buy eight American nuclear reactors, although the two sides disagreed over the reprocessing of spent fuel (which can produce fissile material for bombs).[5] A 1975 US memo articulates the 'serious dilemma [that] we are proposing to Iran more rigorous controls

---

[2] Parisa Hafezi and Hashem Kalantari, 'Khamenei Allies Trounce Ahmadinejad in Iran Election', *Reuters*, 4 March 2012.

[3] Anthony H Cordesman and Khalid R Al-Rodhan, *Iran's Weapons of Mass Destruction: The Real And Potential Threat*, Significant Issues Series, Vol. 28, No. 3 (Washington, DC: Center for Strategic and International Studies, 2006), p. 103.

[4] Ian Anthony, Christer Ahlström and Vitaly Fedchenko, *Reforming Nuclear Export Controls: The Future of the Nuclear Suppliers Group* (Oxford: Oxford University Press, 2007), p. 59.

[5] Sasan Fayazmanesh, *The United States and Iran: Sanctions, Wars and the Policy of Dual Containment* (Abingdon: Routledge, 2008), pp. 124–25.

over plutonium than we have heretofore included in our other agreement, including those with states that are not party to the NPT'.[6] In August 1974, a US National Intelligence Estimate (NIE) observed that Iran was a serious proliferation risk, if trends were to continue.[7] Such cautionary assessments demonstrate that American concern over Iranian nuclear activities is not just a post-revolutionary phenomenon: Washington has been concerned about the dual-use nature of Iranian nuclear activities for over three decades.

At the time, the Shah denied any interest in nuclear weapons. However, there is both circumstantial and other evidence that suggests he wished to retain the flexibility to shift from a civil nuclear to a weapons programme.[8] Indeed, the former head of Iran's atomic energy institute has claimed that his research team had been asked to 'give the country access to all [nuclear] technologies, giving the political decision-makers the possibility of making the appropriate decision and doing so while time permitted them to build a bomb if that is what was required'.[9]

From 1979 to 2001

The 1979 Islamic Revolution affected both the demand and the supply side of Iran's nuclear activities. This section outlines Iran's nuclear activities in the two decades following the revolution, and places them in the context of Iran's broader security concerns.

Ayatollah Khomeini, who deposed the Shah, was opposed to the nuclear programme and cancelled payments to a European enrichment consortium in which Iran had invested. French and German firms withdrew from their projects in Iran, construction of the nuclear power plant at Bushehr was suspended, and the US stopped supplying highly enriched uranium (HEU) for the research reactor. In 1981, Israel destroyed Iraq's Osirak nuclear reactor, mitigating a neighbouring nuclear threat and further reducing Iran's incentive to preserve the policy option of nuclear weapons.[10]

After 1987, the US became directly involved in the so-called 'Tanker War', a subset, between 1984 and 1988, of the broader Iran-Iraq conflict. After attacks on Kuwaiti shipping, the US Navy (and, later, the Soviet navy)

---

[6] National Security Council, 'Report of the NSSM 219: U.S.–Iran Agreement on Cooperation in Civil Uses of Atomic Energy', 14 March 1975, p. 1.

[7] Central Intelligence Agency (CIA), 'Special National Intelligence Estimate: Prospects for Further Proliferation of Nuclear Weapons', 1 April 1974, p. 38.

[8] David Patrikarakos, *Nuclear Iran: The Birth of an Atomic State* (London: I. B. Tauris, 2012), pp. 48–82.

[9] David Albright and Andrea Stricker, 'Iran's Nuclear Program', Iran Primer blog, United States Institute of Peace.

[10] Malfrid Braut-Hegghammer, 'Revisiting Osirak: Preventive Attacks and Nuclear Proliferation Risks', *International Security* (Vol. 36, No. 1, 2011).

began escorting Kuwaiti tankers under a US flag, for instance. Iranian and American forces exchanged fire on multiple occasions, with the US sinking Iranian warships and damaging Iranian oil facilities.[11] The US military presence in the region also grew substantially after the First Gulf War of 1991, with the establishment of bases in Bahrain and Qatar increasing the flexibility and potency of its naval and air power.[12]

Iran decided to resume its nuclear activities at some point in the first half of the 1980s. The Institute for Science and International Security, an American think tank, claims to possess an internal IAEA document from 2009 that says the agency 'was informed [by an unnamed source] that in April 1984 the then President of Iran [now supreme leader], H.E. Ayatollah Khamenei declared, during a meeting of top-echelon political and security officials at the Presidential Palace in Tehran, that the spiritual leader Imam Khomeini had decided to reactivate the nuclear programme [to] serve Iran as a deterrent in the hands of God's soldiers'.[13] In that same month, *Jane's Defence Weekly* reported West German intelligence estimates suggesting that Iran was two years away from completing the development of a bomb with the help of HEU from Pakistan (a claim for which there is no evidence).[14]

Although this timeline is obviously absurd in retrospect, neither these fears nor Iran's alleged ambitions should be particularly surprising. This period coincided with the intensification of the Iran-Iraq War, which itself touched the nuclear programme and heightened Iran's sense of strategic vulnerability in other ways.

Between 1984 and 1988, Iraq attacked Bushehr no fewer than seven times, and in 1982, initiated the use of ballistic missiles against Iran.[15] Only in 1985 did Iran acquire its own such missiles from Libya to respond in kind. In 1988, the so-called 'war of the cities' – a major strategic bombing campaign – saw at least 361 Iraqi missiles launched at Iran, and 117 Iranian missiles fired in the opposite direction.[16] The war was also characterised by the use of chemical weapons: Iraq used mustard gas and a variety of nerve agents, initially inflicting substantial casualties on Iranian forces.[17]

[11] Anthony H Cordesman and Abraham R Wagner, *The Lessons of Modern War, Volume II: The Iran-Iraq War* (Boulder, CO: Westview Press, 1990), ch. 9.
[12] F Gregory Gause, *The International Relations of the Persian Gulf* (Cambridge: Cambridge University Press, 2010), pp. 107, 127, 249.
[13] *Isis-online.org*, 'Internal IAEA Information Links the Supreme Leader to 1984 Decision to Seek a Nuclear Arsenal', 20 April 2012.
[14] *Associated Press*, 'Jane's Believes Iran is Likely to Have N-bomb in 2 Years', 25 April 1985.
[15] Fayazmanesh, *The United States and Iran*, p. 127.
[16] Figures calculated from data in Anthony H Cordesman, *Iran's Military Forces in Transition: Conventional Threats and Weapons of Mass Destruction* (Westport, CT: Greenwood Press, 1999), pp. 223, 294.
[17] Thomas L McNaugher, 'Ballistic Missiles and Chemical Weapons: The Legacy of the Iran-Iraq War', *International Security* (Vol. 15, No. 2, Fall 1990), p. 5.

The very extensive official and non-governmental assistance from Western sources to Iraq's conventional and chemical weaponry, including the US, compounded Iran's belief that Western powers were implacably opposed to the Islamic Republic's survival.[18] That belief had its roots in the years of Western support for the Shah's regime and – despite well-known examples of Iranian co-operation with the United States and Israel – it hardened in the initial confrontations of the post-revolutionary period.

First, Iran's new leaders were embittered at the West's longstanding material and diplomatic support to the autocratic regime of the Shah – at the hands of which leading figures within the Islamic Republic suffered persecution. For example, Iran's present supreme leader, Ayatollah Ali Khamenei, was himself imprisoned in isolation, tortured and exiled to a remote part of the country by the Shah.[19]

These grievances overlapped with an older, even broader set of concerns relating to the West's – and specifically, the American – record of manipulating Iranian domestic politics. These date to the nineteenth century and earlier, when a weakened Iran became an arena for great-power rivalries. However, the most reliably invoked grievance is the American- and British-backed 1953 coup that overthrew the democratically elected government of Mohammad Mosaddegh.[20] In 2000, US Secretary of State Madeleine Albright acknowledged the US role in the coup, admitting that 'it is easy to see now why many Iranians continue to resent this intervention by America in their internal affairs'.[21]

Second, Iran was an avowedly revolutionary government with ambitions extending beyond its borders.[22] The concept of the 'export of revolution' was widely used by Iranian officials, encompassing both 'conventional means of exporting political radicalism – arms, financial support, training, international congresses propaganda and radio programmes', as well as theological means, notably Khomeini's claims that 'the Islamic people were all one and that in Islam there were no

---

[18] Toby Craig Jones, 'America, Oil, and War in the Middle East', *Journal of American History* (Vol. 99, No. 1, 2012); Joost R Hiltermann, *A Poisonous Affair: America, Iraq, and the Gassing of Halabja* (Cambridge: Cambridge University Press, 2007), p. 37.

[19] Karim Sadjadpour, *Reading Khamenei: The World View of Iran's Most Powerful Leader* (Washington, DC: Carnegie Endowment for International Peace, 2009), p. 4.

[20] Ali M Ansari, *Confronting Iran: The Failure of American Foreign Policy and the Roots of Mistrust* (London: C Hurst & Co Publishers, 2006), pp. 87–88.

[21] Madeleine K Albright, 'Remarks Before the American-Iranian Council', speech in Washington, DC, 17 March 2000.

[22] Stephen M Walt, *Revolution and War* (Ithaca, NY: Cornell University Press, 1996), ch. 5.

frontiers', which challenged the territorial integrity and political legitimacy of other Islamic states.[23] Apart from being an ideological commitment, therefore, the export of revolution also served to transfer popular pressure away from the post-revolutionary state and onto external enemies. Cultivating a siege mentality in this way has bolstered citizens' loyalties to a state that has failed to live up to its aspirations.

This transnational vision, in turn, played a role in provoking the Iraqi invasion of Iran, and was in turn reinvigorated by the war itself.[24] The most important strand of this vision proved to be Iran's ability – sometimes contrived, sometimes real – to mobilise Islamic communities, and particularly marginalised Shia communities, outside Iran's borders, often in ways that seemed to challenge the entire political order of the Arab (that is, non-Persian) Middle East.

In turn, the West had its own points of contention with Iran. The first and most embittering was the seizure and detention of sixty-six Americans in the US embassy in Tehran for over a year, which resulted in a failed American rescue attempt and increased prestige for especially anti-American politicians within Iran. As Ali Ansari notes, after this episode, 'the [Iranian] revolution would in large part be defined by its antagonistic relationship with the United States'.[25]

Third, Iran cultivated links to international terrorist groups and extremist movements in Gaza, Iraq, Afghanistan and Lebanon, some of which mounted major attacks on Western or allied – rather than just regional – targets. The most prominent example was the devastating 1983 attack on the US Marine Corps barracks in Beirut, Lebanon, suspected to have been carried out by the Shia Lebanese militant group Hizbullah, an ally and major beneficiary of Iran.[26]

Iran's Lebanese allies took a number of US hostages throughout the 1980s, with the last one being released only in 1991. This had been seen as an area in which Iranian co-operation could beget goodwill, but both sides ended up embittered – the US for the Iranian role in the torture and kidnap of its intelligence and military officers, and Iran because of the perceived ingratitude of the US upon the hostages' release. A national security directive signed by President George H W Bush in October 1989 declared that, as part of a wide range of conditions, the US 'should continue to be prepared for a normal relationship with Iran on the basis of strict reciprocity', but that any 'process of normalization must begin with

---

[23] Fred Halliday, *Islam and the Myth of Confrontation: Religion and Politics in the Middle East*, 2nd ed. (London: I. B. Tauris, 2003), p. 70.
[24] Ali M Ansari, *Modern Iran*, 2nd ed. (Harlow: Pearson Education, 2007), p. 288.
[25] *Ibid.*, p. 227.
[26] Augustus Richard Norton, *Hezbollah: A Short History* (Princeton, NJ: Princeton University Press, 2009), pp. 34–35.

Iranian action to cease its support for international terrorism and help obtain the release of all American hostages'.[27]

These historical grievances should not be exaggerated, as they did not preclude extensive co-operation between the West and Iran in the decades after 1979.[28] In early 1980, for instance, Israel's Prime Minister Menachem Begin approved the shipment of weaponry and spare tyres for Iran's US-made fighter planes, an act that was reciprocated by Iran's permission for the emigration of Iranian Jews.[29]

However, it is clear that nearly all of Iran's post-revolutionary leaders have sought to portray their state as enduring a continuous siege from outside powers and denied its rightful place in the region. This feeds into the nuclear crisis today in multiple ways. In 2005, Iranian President Mahmoud Ahmadinejad compared earlier nuclear agreements reached with the EU to the Russian-imposed Turkmanchai and Golestan treaties of the nineteenth century, which had entailed the loss of substantial Iranian territory including seventeen cities – 'the most humiliating treaties in Iran's history'.[30] Although this was presumably inflated political rhetoric rather than Ahmadinejad's personal conviction, it is suggestive of the degree to which old grievances are perceived to resonate with a modern Iranian audience.

Moreover, the acute US-Iran hostility forged in the immediate aftermath of the revolution has been compounded by reciprocal acts of hostility towards one another. For example, Iran has armed and abetted battlefield adversaries of the US; while the US, in turn, is alleged to have trained the Mujahideen-e-Khalq to mount operations against Iran, despite the US's own classification of the group as a foreign terrorist organisation.[31]

Furthermore, Iran believes that the US does not accept the legitimacy of the Islamic Republic as an entity, and that measures ostensibly designed to solve a specific problem (the nuclear dispute) are in fact intermediate steps towards the forcible overthrow of the regime, in line with past US practice. Since 1979, Iran has had no great-power allies – indeed, since 2006, even Russia and China have acquiesced in its punishment.

Despite this relative isolation, no senior Iranian political figure publicly and clearly advocated the development of nuclear weapons.

---

[27] The White House, 'National Security Directive 26: U.S. Policy Toward the Persian Gulf', 2 October 1989, p. 3.
[28] Multiple examples are given in Dalia Dassa Kaye, Alireza Nader and Parisa Roshan, *Israel and Iran: a Dangerous Rivalry* (Santa Monica, CA: RAND Corporation, 2011), pp. 10–15.
[29] *Ibid.*, pp. 11–14.
[30] Seyed Hossein Mousavian, *The Iranian Nuclear Crisis: A Memoir* (Washington, DC: Carnegie Endowment for International Peace, 2012), p. 190.
[31] Seymour M Hersh, 'Our Men in Iran?', *New Yorker*, 6 April 2012. In September 2012, the Mujahideen-e-Khalq was delisted as a terrorist organisation, following its intensive lobbying effort in the US.

Speaking to the Iranian Revolutionary Guards Corps (IRGC) in October 1988, Hashemi Rafsanjani, then speaker of Iran's parliament, made the argument (which he later recanted) that the need for an Iranian deterrent 'was made very clear during the [Iran-Iraq] war', and urged Iran to 'fully equip ourselves both in the offensive and defensive use of chemical, bacteriological, and radiological weapons'. Notably, he did not advocate the development of nuclear weapons.[32]

What is clear is that Iranian scientists and representatives of the IRGC made contact with the clandestine supply network of Pakistani nuclear scientist A Q Khan in the mid-to-late 1980s. They received blueprints for a P-1 centrifuge and centrifuge components as well as, later, for the more sophisticated P-2 centrifuge.[33] In 1986 and 1987, A Q Khan visited the Bushehr reactor, while American officials have even alleged that Khan provided Iran with a warhead design.[34]

Moreover, in 1987, President Rafsanjani allegedly ordered a feasibility study to examine nuclear weapons and delivery systems.[35] In the same year, Iran also agreed (with tacit US permission) a deal with Argentina worth $5.5 million to receive a new core for the TRR, enabling it to operate with 19.75 per cent-enriched uranium rather than the 90 per cent-enriched (weapons-grade HEU) uranium that was no longer available from the US. Argentina supplied the core in 1998, as well as approximately 150 kg of 19.75 per cent-enriched uranium in 1993.[36] (The exhaustion of this supply is Iran's primary rationale for its enrichment of uranium to 20 per cent today.[37]) Between 1992 and 1995, Iran also signed a series of agreements with Russia that would see Moscow rebuild the Bushehr power plant and provide a light-water reactor.[38]

---

[32] Ray Takeyh, *Guardians of the Revolution: Iran and the World in the Age of the Ayatollahs* (New York: Oxford University Press, 2009), p. 245.
[33] Adrian Levy and Cathy Scott-Clark, *Deception: Pakistan, the United States, and the Secret Trade in Nuclear Weapons* (New York: Walker & Company, 2007), p. 334.
[34] Douglas Jehl, 'C.I.A. Says Pakistanis Gave Iran Nuclear Aid', *New York Times*, 24 November 2004; William J Broad and David E Sanger, 'Report Says Iran Has Data to Make a Nuclear Bomb', *New York Times*, 3 October 2009.
[35] Etel Solingen, *Nuclear Logics: Contrasting Paths in East Asia & the Middle East* (Princeton, NJ: Princeton University Press, 2007), p. 164.
[36] Frank Barnaby, *How Nuclear Weapons Spread: Nuclear-Weapon Proliferation in the 1990s* (Abingdon: Routledge, 2005), p. 99.
[37] Parisa Hafezi, 'Iran to Load Own Nuclear Fuel Rods in Tehran Reactor', *Reuters*, 15 February 2012. Iran has since developed further rationales, such as an implausible interest in a nuclear-powered submarine programme.
[38] John W Parker, *Persian Dreams: Moscow and Tehran Since the Fall of the Shah* (Washington, DC: Potomac Books, 2009), ch. 6; Vladimir A Orlov and Alexander Vinnikov, 'The Great Guessing Game: Russia and the Iranian Nuclear Issue', *Washington Quarterly* (Vol. 28, No. 2, 2005).

Throughout the 1990s, however, the US strongly pressured other states to end this co-operation. Washington persuaded Argentina, India, Spain, Germany, France, Moldova and others to prohibit the sale of nuclear technology to Iran's civilian programme.[39] China discontinued most of its nuclear assistance to Iran by 1997 for this reason.[40] In 1998, Ukraine announced that it would not sell Iran turbines for the Bushehr reactor.

Russia, however, was unwilling to break off assistance completely, despite agreeing not to sell Iran an enrichment facility.[41] As Gordon Corera notes, 'in the mid-1990s Russian engineers and scientists were literally bumping into each other in the streets of Tehran'.[42] This was partly a result of wider shifts in Russian foreign policy: after 1991, Russia grew wary of Turkish intentions, with Moscow especially anxious that Chechen rebels were receiving financial and material assistance from Turkey. Conversely, Turkey grew concerned that Kurdish insurgents were seeking help from Russia. Russia therefore strengthened its ties with Iran.[43]

Russia's fragmented post-Soviet politics were also characterised by competing groups, some of which favoured co-operation with the major industrial states while others – notably those associated with the beleaguered military-industrial complex – advocated deeper ties with former Soviet clients, like Iran, Syria and North Korea.[44]

The US spent much of this decade engaged in ad-hoc counter-proliferation. Washington introduced the Iran-Iraq Arms Nonproliferation Act in 1992, prohibiting the transfer of weapons of mass destruction or missile-related goods and technologies to Iran. The Iran-Libya Sanctions Act (ILSA) of 1996 was even more stringent, as it penalised third-country investors in Libya's energy sector.[45] The ILSA (which a decade later became

---

[39] Chris Hedges, 'Iran May Be Able to Build an Atomic Bomb in 5 Years, U.S. and Israeli Officials Fear', *New York Times*, 5 January 1995.

[40] Anthony, Ahlström and Fedchenko, *Reforming Nuclear Export Controls*, p. 60.

[41] Stuart D Goldman, Kenneth Katzman, Robert D Shuey and Carl E Behrens, 'Russian Missile Technology and Nuclear Reactor Transfers to Iran', Congressional Research Service, 29 July 1998, pp. 12–13.

[42] Gordon Corera, *Shopping for Bombs: Nuclear Proliferation, Global Insecurity, and the Rise and Fall of the A.Q. Khan Network* (Oxford: Oxford University Press, 2006), p. 63.

[43] Fred Halliday, *The Middle East in International Relations: Power, Politics and Ideology* (Cambridge: Cambridge University Press, 2005), p. 136.

[44] Victor Mizin, 'The Russia-Iran Nuclear Connection and U.S. Policy Options', *Middle East Review of International Affairs* (Vol. 8, No. 1, March 2004), p. 75.

[45] Jahangir Amuzegar, 'Iran's Economy and the US Sanctions', *Middle East Journal* (Vol. 51, No. 2, Spring 1997).

the Iran Sanctions Act) was a response to the bombing of a US military facility at Khobar Towers in Saudi Arabia by an IRGC-linked group.[46]

Yet Iran also mellowed in some ways during this period. After becoming president in 1989, Akbar Hashemi Rafsanjani acknowledged that 'Iran needs to stop making enemies'.[47] Rafsanjani understood the economic incentives – particularly, for example, foreign investment in neglected sectors – to improve relations with Western and Arab states. As such, he oversaw the return of American hostages in Lebanon in 1991, adopted less bellicose rhetoric and emphasised post-war reconstruction.[48]

When the Israel-Palestine peace process restarted with the Madrid Conference of 1991, co-sponsored by the US and Soviet Union, Iran was deliberately, and unwisely, excluded, despite Khomeini's expression of interest.[49] Tehran grew concerned that it might be completely cut out by the secular-nationalist Palestine Liberation Organization and, for fear of losing a major source of leverage, strengthened its ties to the more extreme Hamas and Islamic jihad groups, in concert with Syria.[50] This amplified Israeli-Iranian tensions – a process hastened by a domestic shift rightward within Israel, and Iran's growing ballistic-missile capabilities.[51]

Nevertheless, Iran grew less isolated even as it worked to frustrate the evolving Middle Eastern peace process. By 1994, US oil companies had leapfrogged their Japanese counterparts to become Iran's biggest clients.[52] Between October 1990 and 1996, Germany and Iran exchanged more than 300 political, economic, cultural, judicial and parliamentary delegations, with over half involving German and Iranian cabinet ministers.[53]

---

[46] Daniel Byman, *Deadly Connections: States That Sponsor Terrorism* (New York: Cambridge University Press, 2005), p. 108.

[47] Afshin Molavi, 'Iran and the Gulf States', Iran Primer blog, United States Institute of Peace.

[48] David Menashri, *Post-Revolutionary Politics in Iran: Religion, Society and Power* (London: Frank Cass, 2001), p. 67.

[49] Saïd Amir Arjomand, *After Khomeini: Iran Under His Successors* (New York: Oxford University Press, 2009), p. 144.

[50] Iyad Barghouti, 'Palestinian Islamists and the Middle East Peace Conference', *International Spectator* (Vol. 28, No. 1, 1993); Wendy Kristianasen, 'Challenge and Counterchallenge: Hamas's Response to Oslo', *Journal of Palestine Studies* (Vol. 28, No. 3, Spring 1999), pp. 19–36.

[51] Ray Takeyh, 'Iran, Israel and the Politics of Terrorism', *Survival* (Vol. 48, No. 4, 2006), pp. 83–96.

[52] Arjomand, *After Khomeini*, p. 144.

[53] Seyed Hossein Mousavian, *Iran-Europe Relations: Challenges and Opportunities* (Abingdon: Routledge, 2008), p. 2. Admittedly, this rapprochement was not without setbacks. The biggest crisis, until the nuclear file, came in 1996–97 with the conviction of Iranian agents for the assassination of Kurdish-Iranian opposition leaders in Berlin.

Furthermore, between 1990 and 1993, Iran was the second-biggest recipient of credit from Germany's state insurance company.[54] In 1999, Iran restored diplomatic relations with Britain; and by the latter part of the decade, Iran's prolific assassination of dissidents on European soil had tapered off.[55]

Within Iran, the ascendance of reformists, 'a combination of reform-minded clerics and technocratic officials who favour a less oppressive social policy, greater economic liberalisation, a more active civil society and a less confrontational approach to foreign policy', eased this process further.[56] The 1997 election of Mohammad Khatami was particularly significant.[57]

Iran's improved relationship with European states would prove useful in 2003, when EU states took the lead on nuclear diplomacy. However, much of this normalisation was reversed in the years after 2006, when European states spearheaded the enactment of sanctions, and particularly from late 2011, following the intensification of European economic pressure on Iran, the state-sanctioned storming by crowds of the British embassy in Tehran, and the retaliatory closure of the British and other European embassies.[58]

These changes took place amidst a wider US rebalancing in the region. After the revolution in 1979, the US had imposed broad sanctions on Iran. During the 1980s, the US provided support to both sides in the Iran-Iraq War, but leaned towards Iraq for fear of Iran's avowed revolutionary agenda and complicity in acts of terrorism against US forces and interests. In the 1990s, this evolved into a policy of 'dual containment', which Ray Takeyh and Suzanne Maloney describe 'as part of a broader reconceptualization of a post-Soviet strategic landscape dominated by threats from rogue states [in contrast] with the historic tendency to balance one of the northern Gulf states against the other'.[59]

---

[54] Mousavian, *The Iranian Nuclear Crisis*, p. 438.
[55] James Dobbins, Alireza Nader, Dalia Dassa Kaye and Frederic Wehrey, *Coping with a Nuclearizing Iran* (Santa Monica, CA: RAND Corporation, 2011), p. 67.
[56] Peter Jones, 'Succession and the Supreme Leader in Iran', *Survival* (Vol. 53, No. 6, 2011), p. 109.
[57] Matthew C Wells, 'Thermidor in the Islamic Republic of Iran: The Rise of Muhammad Khatami', *British Journal of Middle Eastern Studies* (Vol. 26, No. 1, 1999); Ray Takeyh, 'Iran at a Crossroads', *Middle East Journal* (Vol. 57, No. 1, Winter 2003).
[58] Rick Gladstone and Nicholas Kulish, 'West Tightens Iran Sanctions After Embassy Attack', *New York Times*, 1 December 2011.
[59] Ray Takeyh and Suzanne Maloney, 'The Self-Limiting Success of Iran Sanctions', *International Affairs* (Vol. 87, No. 6, 2011), p. 1301.

Despite these constraints, Iran made important advances in its uranium-mining and conversion capabilities, heavy-water reactor and heavy-water production plant projects, and – what would prove to be most contentious – uranium-enrichment activity.

Throughout the period from 1979 to 2001, concerns persisted that Iran was seeking nuclear weapons. In 1992, a CIA report concluded that 'Iran is making progress on a nuclear arms program and could develop a nuclear weapon by 2000', with a senior nuclear official in the Clinton administration judging that 'Iran has powerful political incentives for developing nuclear weapons and is trying to develop a broad-based nuclear infrastructure that it hopes will give them the option for weapons if they decide to exercise it'.[60] A 1995 report in the *New York Times* was headlined 'Iran May Be Able to Build an Atomic Bomb in 5 Years, U.S. and Israeli Officials Fear', and quoted a 'senior official' as warning that if 'Iran is not interrupted in this program by some foreign power, it will have the device in more or less five years'.[61] In 1998, a CIA report to Congress declared that 'Iran is seeking to develop an indigenous capability to produce various types of nuclear, chemical, and biological weapons and their delivery systems'.[62]

From 2001 to 2012

After the terrorist attacks of 11 September 2001, a series of important changes took place in the regional and global security environment, creating a partial convergence of American and Iranian interests on issues ranging from Al-Qa'ida to Saddam Hussein's regime in Iraq and the Taliban regime in Afghanistan. However, this period also saw the public exposure of clandestine nuclear sites within Iran, and the shift in political influence to hard-liners in Washington and Tehran.

Partial Convergence of Interests
First, the onset of the campaign formerly known as the Global War on Terror shifted the focus of the US and allied governments to international terrorism, with a particular emphasis on Al-Qa'ida in Afghanistan and

---

[60] Elaine Sciolino, 'C.I.A. Says Iran Makes Progress on Atom Arms', *New York Times*, 30 November 1992.
[61] Hedges, 'Iran May Be Able to Build an Atomic Bomb in 5 Years'; from the same year, see Shahram Chubin, 'Does Iran Want Nuclear Weapons?', *Survival* (Vol. 37, No. 1, Spring 1995).
[62] CIA, 'Unclassified Report to Congress on the Acquisition of Technology Relating to Weapons of Mass Destruction and Advanced Conventional Munitions', 1998.

Pakistan. Iran, a Shia-majority country with a Shia clerical leadership, was naturally opposed to Al-Qa'ida's extreme Sunni ideology.[63]

Second, the US-led invasion of Afghanistan deposed the Taliban, a strategic adversary of Iran. The momentary convergence of interests enabled some fruitful, if ephemeral, US-Iranian co-operation against mutual threats in western Afghanistan. In 1998, the Taliban had killed eleven Iranian diplomats in the northern Afghan city of Mazar-e-Sharif, prompting Iran to mobilise troops on the border. Moreover, Taliban massacres of Afghan Shia Muslims had also prompted anger among the people and officials of Iran alike.[64] In the 1990s, Iran, with India and Russia, had provided assistance to the non-Pashtun, mainly Dari- or Persian-speaking Afghan minorities, unified under the banner of the Northern Alliance, against the mainly Pashtun, Pashto-speaking Taliban.[65]

Barnett Rubin, a political scientist and now senior adviser to the US special representative for Afghanistan and Pakistan, observed a very high degree of US-Iranian co-operation 'both in the field, in Tajikistan and Afghanistan, and in diplomacy, where … members of the [IRGC] cooperated with the CIA and US Special Operations Forces in supplying and funding the commanders of the Northern Alliance'. Perhaps most remarkably, 'Iranian officials later offered to work under US command to assist in building the Afghan National Army'.[66] At the same time, Iran's policy was not entirely coherent. Even impartial Afghan officials agree with British and American officials that the Quds Force of the IRGC – tasked with overseas special operations, including liaison with militant groups – later extended limited help to parts of the insurgency against Western and Afghan National Army troops in Afghanistan.[67]

Although these instances of co-operation might have been developed into something more, the US did not take advantage as it might have done. James Dobbins, a former diplomat who led the US delegation at negotiations leading to Afghanistan's 2001 Bonn Agreement, notes that 'in 2002 and again in 2003, Washington actually spurned offers from Tehran to cooperate on Afghanistan and Iraq and negotiate out other US/Iranian differences, including over its nuclear program'. Dobbins adds that the Iranian government 'nevertheless persisted in offering cooperation

---

[63] Leah Farrall, 'Interview with a Taliban Insider: Iran's Game in Afghanistan', *Atlantic Monthly*, 14 November 2011.
[64] Emile Hokayem, 'Chapter Eight: Iran', in *Afghanistan: To 2015 and Beyond*, Adelphi Series (Vol. 51, No. 425–26, 2011).
[65] Mohsen M Milani, 'Iran's Policy Towards Afghanistan', *Middle East Journal* (Vol. 60, No. 2, 2006).
[66] Barnett R Rubin and Sara Batmanglich, 'The US and Iran in Afghanistan: Policy Gone Awry', MIT Center for International Studies, October 2008, p. 3.
[67] *Ibid.*, p. 4.

on Afghanistan, proposing to help to train Afghan forces fighting the Taliban, an offer not taken up'.[68]

Third, the invasion of Iraq in 2003 altered Iran's strategic predicament by removing another adversarial Sunni government: that of Saddam Hussein. Many of Iraq's Shia elites who benefited from regime change – including the incumbent prime minister, Nuri Al-Maliki – had previously lived in exile in Iran, had extensive ties to Iran's clerical establishment, and were perceived in the US as being under a high degree of Iranian influence. Indeed, the non-partisan US Congressional Research Service acknowledged that 'Iran's overall goals in Iraq have differed little from the main emphasis of US policy – establishing a democratic process that reflects majority preferences and thereby empowers potential Shiite allies'.[69]

In 2005, Saudi Arabia's foreign minister, Prince Saud Al-Faisal, lamented that 'we fought a war together to keep Iran from occupying Iraq after Iraq was driven out of Kuwait. Now we are handing the whole country over to Iran without reason'.[70] As in Afghanistan, Iran funded and abetted armed groups in order to preserve influence, gather intelligence and impose tactical costs on the occupying American forces. After the March 2010 elections, the most significant Iraqi candidates for public office openly travelled to Tehran for consultations with the Iranian government.[71] Iran also played a key role in brokering a ceasefire, by persuading the Shia cleric Muqtada Al-Sadr to stop attacks by his militia on Iraqi security forces.[72]

In one sense, regime change in Iraq collapsed the premise of 'dual containment' by eliminating one of the policy's two targets; in another sense, the growth of Iranian influence, even perceived tutelage, over Iraq simply shifted the tactical and operational form of that containment. Regime change in Iraq had created yet another theatre in which the US would have to counter agents of Iran, reinforcing the rationale for a forward deployment of US forces.

At the same time, the presence of large numbers of US forces, peaking at nearly 170,000 at the height of the so-called 'surge', concerned Iran, particularly given its inclusion in President George W Bush's 'axis of

---

[68] Dobbins, Nader, Kaye and Wehrey, *Coping with a Nuclearizing Iran*, pp. 4–8.
[69] Christopher M Blanchard, Kenneth Katzman, Carol Migdalovitz and Jeremy Sharp, 'Iraq: Regional Perspectives and U.S. Policy', Congressional Research Service, 6 October 2009, p. 8.
[70] Vali Nasr, *The Shia Revival: How Conflicts within Islam Will Shape the Future* (New York: W. W. Norton & Company, 2006), p. 242.
[71] Rod Nordland, 'Iran Plays Host to Delegations After Iraq Elections', *New York Times*, 1 April 2010.
[72] Mohammed Tawfeeq and Jonathan Wald, 'Sources: Iran Helped Prod Al-Sadr Cease-fire', *CNN*, 31 March 2008.

evil' in early 2002, scarcely months after the US-Iranian co-operation documented above. Iran's fears would recede, and its confidence would grow in the following years, as it became clearer that the US forces on Iran's flanks would be mired in inconclusive counter-insurgency efforts, and would not be especially free to threaten Iran without compromising their military objectives within Iraq and Afghanistan.

Domestic Political Transformation

Fourth, there was a change in the balance of power within both Iran and the United States. In Iran, power shifted away from the reformist camp, which had dominated under President Mohammad Khatami after 1997, to a group of hard-liners under President Mahmoud Ahmadinejad, elected in 2005.[73] Ali Ansari notes that 'as the reformists were increasingly marginalised, the battle for political control shifted to [within] the Right, between the moderate and hardline conservatives', with the latter winning out in a series of elections between 2003 and 2005.[74] Ahmadinejad is often associated with part of this group, the principlists, who 'advocate a return to the doctrines and teachings of Khomeini, are deeply suspicious of social and political liberalisation [and] profess to be suspicious of any opening of relations with the West' – in contrast to Khatami's reformists or Rafsanjani's 'pragmatic conservatives'.[75]

The nuclear dispute and Arab fears of an Iranian-backed 'Shia crescent' had both flared up before Ahmadinejad's election. However, concerns surrounding these two issues have certainly worsened during his tenure. For instance, Iran's uranium-enrichment programme was restarted in early 2006.[76] Writing in his memoirs about his first meeting with Ahmadinejad, the former head of Iran's delegation to the IAEA, Seyed Hossein Mousavian, noted that 'he [Ahmadinejad] told me in clear terms that he did not care about the IAEA resolutions, nor the possible referral of the nuclear file to the UN Security Council. He even said he would welcome sanctions by the international community because these sanctions [would force] the country to become more independent and self-sufficient'.[77]

---

[73] Ali Gheissari and Vali Nasr, 'The Conservative Consolidation in Iran', *Survival* (Vol. 47, No. 2, 2005).
[74] Ansari, *Modern Iran*, p. 334.
[75] Jones, 'Succession and the Supreme Leader in Iran', p. 108.
[76] However, the Isfahan uranium-conversion facility was reactivated and its IAEA seals removed 'in the last days of the Khatami presidency'. See Mousavian, *The Iranian Nuclear Crisis*, p. 179.
[77] Barbara Slavin, 'Former Iranian Negotiator Faults His Nation's Nuclear Diplomacy', *Al-Monitor*, 6 June 2012.

At the same time, the neoconservative foreign policy of the George W Bush administration, and its transformative vision for the Middle East in particular, limited opportunities for co-operation and greatly heightened mutual US-Iranian threat perceptions, even if the most ambitious facets of that policy had been shed or toned down by 2006.[78]

Ambassador James Dobbins recalls perhaps the most significant lost opportunity: 'shortly after the US invasion of Iraq, the Iranian regime passed to Washington [through Swiss channels] an even more comprehensive offer [than the ones documented above] to negotiate out all outstanding US-Iranian differences. Again this initiative was ignored'.[79] The then-US Secretary of State Condoleezza Rice acknowledged that 'what the Iranians wanted ... was to be one-on-one with the United States so that this could be about the United States and Iran', although she later denied having ever seen the relevant letter.[80]

US officials, along with those of allied countries, had for some time complained that Iranian guidance, weaponry and funding were strengthening insurgents in Afghanistan and Iraq, and that Iranian assistance to other non-state armed groups – notably, Hamas and Hizbullah – was unrelenting. As such, Iran's proposals were deemed not to be sincere or plausible.[81] Former Deputy Secretary of State Richard L Armitage claimed that the administration 'couldn't determine what was the Iranians' and what was the Swiss ambassador's' in the memo, and that the Iranians 'were trying to put too much on the table' for effective negotiations.[82]

Nonetheless, episodes like this one may have affected Iranian perceptions of American sincerity in negotiations, not least because, instead of merely declining Iran's offer, the administration instead rebuked the Swiss intermediaries for exceeding their remit.[83]

Nuclear Revelations
This set of changes – the transformation of Iran's security environment, rapid flux in the US-Iran relationship, and wrenching domestic changes

---

[78] Robert Jervis, 'Understanding the Bush Doctrine', *Political Science Quarterly* (Vol. 118, No. 3, 2003), pp. 369–84.
[79] Dobbins, Nader, Kaye and Wehrey, *Coping with a Nuclearizing Iran*, pp. 7–8.
[80] Glenn Kessler, 'Rice Denies Seeing Iranian Proposal in '03', *Washington Post*, 8 February 2007.
[81] Author interviews with retired British and American officials, Washington, DC and London, April and July 2012.
[82] Glenn Kessler, '2003 Memo Says Iranian Leaders Backed Talks', *Washington Post*, 14 February 2007.
[83] Parsi, *A Single Roll of the Dice*, Kindle edition, location 189 (ch. 1).

within both countries – provide the context in which to understand the diplomacy surrounding Iran's nuclear programme after 2001.

In 2002, an exiled Iranian opposition group publicly revealed, almost certainly on the basis of American intelligence that had been previously shared with the IAEA, hitherto clandestine elements of Iran's nuclear programme.[84] These comprised a uranium-enrichment plant and research laboratory at Natanz, and a heavy-water production plant at Arak, both capable of facilitating the production of fissile material for nuclear weapons. Iran had been a non-proliferation concern in the preceding years anyway. The 2002 US Nuclear Posture Review had invoked Iranian behaviour as a factor in US nuclear policy and, in 2000, the CIA had told US policy-makers that it could not rule out the possibility that Iran had acquired nuclear weapons with foreign assistance.[85] Nevertheless, the revelation of these secret sites represented the beginning of the crisis in its present form.

The diplomatic response came in several phases. These grew progressively more coercive in their approach to Iran, punctuated by a few periods of engagement.

First, in October 2003, France, the UK and Germany (the 'EU3') extracted a pledge from Iran to disclose its nuclear activities, sign and ratify the Additional Protocol (AP) to its Safeguards Agreement with the IAEA (thereby permitting more intrusive inspections), and suspend enrichment activities – all in exchange for civil nuclear co-operation.[86] Russian work on the Bushehr reactor continued apace, despite American misgivings. Nonetheless, Iran signed the AP that December. Although Iran voluntarily implemented it for years, it never ratified the protocol, and swiftly disavowed it after IAEA reports documented and criticised the various ways in which Iran's alleged nuclear activities had violated reporting obligations.

According to the best estimate of the US intelligence community, made with 'high confidence', it was during 2003 that Iran halted its nuclear-weapons programme and redirected it to less sensitive, dual-use activities.[87] However, there is disagreement over whether, when and which aspects of the programme may have been later resumed. In 2009, a German federal court cited a May 2008 report from Germany's foreign intelligence service, saying that the agency had 'showed comprehensively' that 'development work on nuclear weapons can be observed in Iran even

---

[84] Levy and Scott-Clark, *Deception*, pp. 332–35.
[85] US Department of Defense, 'Nuclear Posture Review Report', 8 January 2002, p. 16; James Risen with Judith Miller, 'C.I.A. Tells Clinton An Iranian A-Bomb Can't be Ruled Out', *New York Times*, 17 January 2000.
[86] Nazila Fathi, 'Iran Signs Inspection Pact on Atomic Sites', *New York Times*, 18 December 2003.
[87] US National Intelligence Council, 'National Intelligence Estimate – Iran: Nuclear Intentions and Capabilities', November 2007.

after 2003', a claim that is corroborated only by a few, controversial pieces of evidence cited in IAEA reports.[88] More recently, senior US and Israeli officials have reaffirmed the conclusion of the 2007 NIE that Iran has not yet decided to build nuclear weapons, even if it preserves the option of doing so by keeping facilities dormant and individuals inactive. Regardless of what happened to Iran's alleged weapons programme, then, broader nuclear activities certainly did not stop.

The second phase of diplomacy came with the Paris Agreement of November 2004, wherein Iran suspended enrichment activities (it had not yet begun the actual enrichment of uranium) in exchange for promises of trade and aid. The EU3 later offered security guarantees against an invasion of Iran, nuclear fuel and civil nuclear technology. These were offered in return for: a *permanent* suspension of enrichment and associated nuclear activities; a dismantling of the heavy-water reactor at Arak (capable of producing plutonium for weapons); a promise to allow inspections without prior notice (going beyond the demands of the AP, which is less stringent); and a promise that Iran would not exercise its legal right to withdraw from the NPT.

However, days after Ahmadinejad assumed the presidency in August 2005, Iran 'broke' the IAEA seals at its Isfahan facility and resumed uranium conversion (a process that precedes uranium enrichment) – something that Iran's parliament had been urging. Iran's official rationale was that it had not been offered sufficient inducements to continue its moratorium on enrichment, dismissing the carrots on offer as 'insulting and humiliating'.[89] However, in private, EU diplomats complained that, without US involvement, there was 'simply nothing of substance they could offer Iran'.[90]

Even after this, the EU3 held out a new deal, which would have involved Iran permanently halting most of its fuel production. However, in September 2005, the IAEA Board of Governors declared Iran to be in formal non-compliance of its NPT Safeguards Agreement and, in February 2006, took the major step of referring the issue to the UN Security Council. This was a significant escalation of the crisis, and one that transplanted predominantly European diplomacy onto the global stage and deeply worried Iranian decision-makers.[91] This step ensured that further pressure on Iran would have at least some legal sanction and greater force.

---

[88] Bruno Schirra, 'Germany's Spies Refuted the 2007 NIE Report', *Wall Street Journal*, 20 July 2009.
[89] *Guardian*, 'Iran Urged to Re-suspend Uranium Enrichment', 11 August 2005.
[90] David Patrikarakos, 'Why This Round of Iran Nuclear Talks is Different', *Haaretz*, 4 May 2012.
[91] Hassan Rowhani, 'Beyond the Challenges Facing Iran and the IAEA Concerning the Nuclear Dossier', speech to the Supreme Cultural Revolution Council, trans. FBIS, *Rahbord*, 30 September 2005, pp. 8–13, <http://lewis.armscontrolwonk.com/files/2012/08/Rahbord.pdf>, accessed 19 October 2012.

This, the third and first truly *coercive* phase of diplomacy, began in March 2006 with the Security Council's issuance of a thirty-day deadline for Iran to cease enrichment activity and the formation, in June, of the so-called P5 + 1 as the umbrella group for engagement with Iran. This group comprised all five permanent members of the UN Security Council in addition to Germany – a significant step given that previously the US had only influenced talks at a distance, and Russia and China had been peripheral.

A fuller accounting of this period somewhat undercuts the widely held idea that Iran's interlocutors have never offered it inducements. In the spring of 2007, the P5 + 1, as a bloc, offered Iran a raft of upgraded incentives. These included an easing of longstanding US sanctions on Iran's civil aviation, a five-year supply of nuclear fuel, a light-water nuclear reactor, an 'energy partnership' with the EU, what was explicitly called a 'regional security forum for the Persian Gulf' and, perhaps most importantly, the prospect of allowing Iran to resume enrichment at a later date. The alternative was toughened sanctions.[92] In short, the P5 + 1 offered bigger carrots and bigger sticks.

In hindsight, this was a pivotal moment. Iran had restarted enrichment in April 2006, ending a three-year suspension. It only replied to the P5 + 1 offer months later and did not agree to stop enrichment. By that month, the UN Security Council had voted, nearly unanimously – with only Qatar abstaining – to give Iran until the end of August to stop enrichment. When it had not done so by December, the Security Council imposed the first of what would become multiple rounds of sanctions and extensions of the deadline for suspending enrichment.

Each of these was ineffective in compelling Iran to cease enrichment, and each prompted increasingly onerous sanctions by both the EU and the UN Security Council over the following several years. These were matched with expanded incentives, such as more political co-operation, additional energy assistance, and the offer of a 'freeze for freeze', entailing a freeze of sanctions in exchange for a freeze on enrichment expansion. Some small compromises were reached, such as Iran's agreement with the IAEA in August 2007 to clear up 'outstanding questions', but these bore little fruit.

The IAEA formulated two sets of outstanding questions. One dealt with the ostensibly civilian nuclear-energy side of Iran's activities, and the second with possible military dimensions. The Iranians, and a number of individuals involved from the IAEA, will admit that Iran did much to address the first set of questions. However, Iran refused to go into possible military dimensions, resulting in considerable acrimony. This was an

---

[92] This 'package' is documented in UN Security Council Resolution 1747.

important development in Iran's relationship with the IAEA and the P5 + 1.[93]

The fourth phase of diplomacy might be dated to 2009, when a series of important changes took place.

First, the new Obama administration promised a greater commitment to engagement with Iran. Second, this commitment was almost immediately complicated following Iran's disputed presidential elections in the summer by domestic protests and corresponding repression. Third, it was revealed that Iran had covertly begun to build another enrichment site, Fordow, under a mountain near the holy city of Qom.[94]

There is some debate as to whether Iran was in violation of its earlier agreements with the IAEA by failing to declare this site. Under Code 3.1 of Iran's Subsidiary Arrangements with the IAEA, Iran was bound to declare the construction of new facilities 'normally no later than 180 days before the facility is scheduled to receive nuclear material for the first time'. This would put Iran in the clear over Qom. However, in the early 1990s the IAEA had established a 'modified Code 3.1', requiring that states declare the intended construction and design of new facilities as soon as a decision is taken. Iran agreed to the change in February 2003, in the early stages of nuclear diplomacy with the West, but in 2007 announced that it was reverting to the earlier version.

Critics contend that the decision to build Qom was taken while Iran was still under the modified code and that therefore Iran breached its obligations. Moreover, it is claimed that Iran was not legally entitled to unilaterally repudiate parts of its Safeguards Agreement.[95] Others, however, argue that the Subsidiary Arrangements do not constitute a treaty, and that Iran was, and remains, only legally bound by the less stringent conditions spelt out in the more general Safeguards Agreement.[96]

This legal debate may be largely irrelevant: in reality, the discovery of a clandestine site further poisoned the atmosphere. Western states view Iran's behaviour as violating *at least* the spirit of its earlier agreements, and therefore indicative of its opaque intentions and obstructionist behaviour.

Fourth, despite these challenges, the P5 + 1 came close to reaching a temporary settlement with Iran in late 2009, whereby Iran would export 75 per cent of its LEU at that time (1,200 kg – approximately the quantity that, if further enriched, would suffice for one bomb) to Russia, in return for

---

[93] I am grateful to Andrea Berger for clarifying these points.
[94] David E Sanger and William J Broad, 'U.S. and Allies Warn Iran Over Nuclear "Deception"', *New York Times*, 25 September 2009.
[95] James M Acton, 'Iran Violated International Obligations on Qom Facility', *Carnegie Endowment for International Peace*, 25 September 2009.
[96] Daniel Joyner, 'The Qom Enrichment Facility: Was Iran Legally Bound to Disclose?', *Jurist*, 5 March 2010.

reactor fuel. Had these negotiations been successful, it would have taken Iran ten months to replenish this amount of LEU, buying time for further negotiations.[97] However, despite the positive reaction from Iranian negotiators and Ahmadinejad's assertion that he 'did not have a problem' with the deal, it foundered on opposition from elites across the Iranian political spectrum.[98]

Parliamentary speaker and former nuclear negotiator Ali Larijani, secretary of the Expediency Council Mohsen Rezaei, and then-presidential candidate and later Green Movement leader Mir Hossein Mousavi all criticised the swap. Ayatollah Khamenei, likely taking into account this political backlash, also opposed the deal and thereby killed it.[99] A former Iranian nuclear negotiator attributes this failure to the fact that 'the Geneva agreement was made public before President Ahmadinejad and negotiators had time to explain the deal and win over conservatives and Iran's Supreme National Security Council'.[100] It may also have been the case that, as Mark Fitzpatrick suggests, 'the positive Western media reaction ... made Iranians naturally suspicious'.[101] Iran later offered to send its LEU to Kish Island, an Iranian island with free-trade-zone status in the Gulf, but this would have left the material vulnerable to confiscation.[102]

Brazil and Turkey resurrected this approach in the following year's so-called 'Tehran declaration', which proposed a similar swap and secured Tehran's agreement.[103] However, the US and others rejected this for a variety of reasons: Iran's stockpile had grown in the interim; there was no restriction on Iran's enrichment to 20 per cent (which had begun that year); and the deal was open-ended.[104] Most importantly, the P5 + 1 (which excludes Brazil and Turkey) had been working on a new sanctions resolution during which Washington had made significant efforts to secure the co-operation of both Russia and China, and for this reason it was

[97] Mark Fitzpatrick, 'Iran: The Fragile Promise of the Fuel-Swap Plan', *Survival* (Vol. 52, No. 3, 2010).
[98] David E Sanger, 'Both Iran and West Fear a Trap on Deal', *New York Times*, 25 October 2009.
[99] Mark Fitzpatrick, 'Containing the Iranian Nuclear Crisis: The Useful Precedent of a Fuel Swap', *Perceptions* (Vol. 16, No. 2, Summer 2011), p. 15.
[100] International Crisis Group, 'In Heavy Waters: Iran's Nuclear Program, the Risk of War and Lessons from Turkey', Middle East and Europe Report No. 116, February 2012, p. 11.
[101] Fitzpatrick, 'Containing the Iranian Nuclear Crisis', p. 21.
[102] Fitzpatrick, 'Iran', p. 74.
[103] Diego Santos Vieira de Jesus, 'Building Trust and Flexibility: A Brazilian View of the Fuel Swap with Iran', *Washington Quarterly* (Vol. 34, No. 2, 2011); Delphine Strauss and David Gardner, 'Turkey: The Sentinel Swivels', *Financial Times*, 20 July 2010.
[104] *Reuters*, 'Powers Dismiss Iran Fuel Offer Before U.N. Vote', 9 June 2010.

concerned that any delay in imposing sanctions would imperil the hard-won political resolve needed to secure multilateral pressure on Iran.

Towards the end of 2009, American diplomats in Vienna had privately concluded that Iran's rejection of the first swap deal and its 'refusal to pursue engagement on the nuclear issue with the P5 + 1, leaves us no choice but to ratchet up the pressure in hopes of prompting a change of calculus in Tehran'.[105] Separately, US intelligence officials concluded on the basis of 'message traffic between Ayatollah Khamenei and other power centres inside the country' that 'it was the supreme leader himself who killed this whole thing [the deal to swap Iranian LEU for reactor fuel]', perhaps explaining why American officials were so sceptical of further Turkish and Brazilian efforts.[106]

As such, a fourth round of UN and bilateral talks were imposed in the summer of 2010. The P5 + 1 met with Iran in December 2010 and again in January 2011. Western states saw the latter meeting as especially frustrating, because Iran considered the removal of all sanctions to be a precondition for talking about nuclear matters.[107]

The fifth and most coercive phase of diplomacy yet began at the end of 2011 and the beginning of 2012, with the imposition of punitive economic sanctions on Iran. This was enabled, in part, by the release in November 2011 of one of the IAEA's most cautionary reports on Iran to date, which documented 'possible military dimensions' to Iran's nuclear programme, including some new pieces of suggestive evidence.[108]

That same month, Britain had used its 2008 Counter-Terrorism Act to compel its credit and financial institutions to cease all transactions with Iranian banks, including the Central Bank of Iran (CBI).[109] Then, at the end of December 2011, President Obama signed into law sanctions on any financial institution worldwide that did business with the CBI, thereby blocking payments for oil.[110] Although the bill allowed for some exemptions, such as for states demonstrating efforts to cut their purchases of Iranian oil, it nevertheless represented a significant escalation. At the end of January 2012, the EU imposed a similarly

---

[105] US embassy, 'US Embassy Cable – 2010: Vienna's Year of Iran?', Vienna, 16 December 2009, <http://cables.mrkva.eu/cable.php?id = 240210>, accessed 19 October 2012. Note that this cable was written before the swap deal collapsed.
[106] David E Sanger, *Confront and Conceal: Obama's Secret Wars and Surprising Use of American Power* (New York: Crown, 2012), p. 185.
[107] Scott Peterson, 'Why Iran Nuclear Talks Ended in Stalemate', *Christian Science Monitor*, 22 January 2011.
[108] Director General of the IAEA, GOV/2011/65, 'Implementation of the NPT Safeguards Agreement and Relevant Provisions of Security Council Resolutions in the Islamic Republic of Iran', IAEA, 8 November 2011.
[109] *BBC News*, 'UK Severs Ties with Iranian Banks', 22 November 2011.
[110] Laura MacInnis, 'U.S. Imposes Sanctions on Banks Dealing with Iran', *Reuters*, 1 January 2012.

unprecedented oil embargo on Iran and, in March, Iran was cut off from a major international banking system, SWIFT.[111]

The objective of these most recent sanctions is not to choke *all* Iranian oil exports entirely, but to limit the volume sold and force Iran to sell oil at a discount, as a result of increasingly oligopsonistic conditions (that is, conditions favouring the buyers as a result of a shrunken market), and therefore shrink its revenue. The intention was partly to limit the flow of resources into the nuclear programme and, more importantly, to impose a strategic cost on Iran that would compel it to make greater concessions in negotiations. The EU foreign policy high representative, Catherine Ashton, claimed that the intention was 'to put pressure on Iran to come back to the negotiating table'.[112]

Iran's Present Nuclear Status

Nuclear weapons comprise three things: fissile material, which can be HEU or plutonium; a warhead that triggers a nuclear explosion of this fissile material; and a delivery system to transport the warhead to its target. Over the past twenty-five years, Iran has made progress on all three fronts, although the second – the warhead itself – remains an area of dispute amongst officials and analysts.

The heavy-water reactor which is under construction at Arak is scheduled to be operational in late 2014, at which point any military strike against it could result in serious radioactive contamination. The reprocessing of spent fuel from such a reactor can produce plutonium for bombs. Plutonium undergoes fission more readily than uranium, allowing for warheads with better yield-to-weight ratios, which are therefore easier to fit onto ballistic missiles.[113] However, although this may become a more sensitive issue over the next year, the international community is currently focused on Iran's uranium-enrichment programme.

Since the end of 2011, Iran has rapidly increased its pace of enrichment, as well as its unused enrichment capacity. Iran's stockpile of MEU, enriched to 20 per cent, leapt up by nearly three quarters between February and August 2012. MEU, which Iran began producing only two years ago, is of particular concern because it is – somewhat counterintuitively – nine-tenths of the way to the creation of weapons-grade uranium. This is because enrichment involves removing unwanted isotopes from uranium (U-238) and leaving useful, fissile ones (U-235). The

---

[111] Rick Gladstone and Stephen Castle, 'Global Network Expels as Many as 30 of Iran's Banks in Move to Isolate its Economy', *New York Times*, 15 March 2012.
[112] *BBC News*, 'EU Iran Sanctions: Ministers Adopt Iran Oil Imports Ban', 23 January 2012.
[113] Frank Barnaby, *How Nuclear Weapons Spread*, p. 33.

majority of unwanted isotopes have been removed at the point when uranium has been enriched to 20 per cent, leaving a far smaller amount to remove in order for the uranium to be enriched to 90 per cent. (See Figure 1 for a graphical representation of this.)

It is important to note that, as of the IAEA's August report, Iran has converted or is converting over half of its total stockpile of MEU to make reactor fuel.[114] This is a reversible process until the fuel is actually used in the reactor – thus far, only a very small amount has actually been irradiated in this way.[115] Nonetheless, Israeli Defense Minister Ehud Barak acknowledged in October 2012 that Iran's use of MEU for reactor fuel, by shrinking its immediately accessible stockpile, 'allows contemplating delaying the moment of truth by eight to 10 months'.[116] This indicates something important: for Israel, only uranium in enrichable chemical form is of concern when calculating the timeline for any Iranian effort at building a nuclear weapon. The IAEA's November 2012 report suggests that Iran is no longer converting MEU to non-enrichable form, but it could resume doing so at any point if it wished to lessen the sense of crisis.[117]

Iran's present stocks of MEU, if further enriched, are likely insufficient for one bomb. However, more sophisticated warhead designs and acceptance of lower yields would allow a bomb to be made with less than the 25 kg of HEU usually assumed to be necessary; indeed, one widely used estimate is 15 kg, although others suggest as little as 4 kg would suffice for better-designed weapons with lower yields.[118]

If Iran's leaders decided to rush to produce a bomb today (something called 'breakout'), how long would it take?

In January 2012, US Defense Secretary and former CIA Director Leon Panetta said: 'the consensus is that, if [Iran] decided to do it, it would probably take them about a year to be able to produce a bomb and then possibly another one to two years in order to put it on a deliverable vehicle

[114] Director General of the IAEA, GOV/2012/23, 'Implementation of the NPT Safeguards Agreement and Relevant Provisions of Security Council Resolutions in the Islamic Republic of Iran', IAEA, 25 May 2012, p. 3.
[115] David Albright and Christina Walrond, 'Iranian Production of 19.75 Percent Enriched Uranium: Beyond its Realistic Needs', ISIS Report, 15 June 2012, pp. 6–7.
[116] David Blair, 'Israel says Iran has Pulled Back from the Brink of Nuclear Weapon – For Now', *Daily Telegraph*, 30 October 2012.
[117] Fredrik Dahl, 'U.N.'s Nuclear Report on Iran May not be All Bad News for West', *Reuters*, 14 November 2012.
[118] For the higher and lower estimates see, respectively, David Albright, Frans Berkhout and William Walker, *World Inventory of Plutonium and Highly Enriched Uranium, 1992* (New York: Oxford University Press, 1993), p. 66; Thomas B Cochran, 'The Problem of Nuclear Energy Proliferation', in Patrick L Clawson (ed.), *Energy and National Security in the 21st Century* (Washington, DC: National Defense University, 1995), p. 98.

Figure 1: Effort required in relation to the enrichment level of U-235.

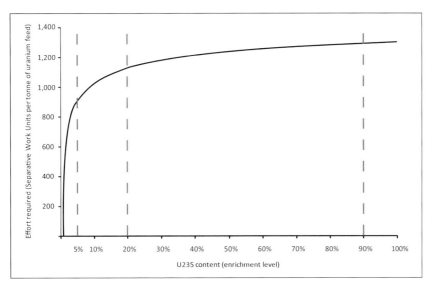

Source: Adapted from World Nuclear Association, 'Uranium Enrichment', September 2012, < www.world-nuclear.org/info/inf28.html >, accessed 20 November 2012.

of some sort in order to deliver that weapon'.[119] In September 2012, Panetta updated this projection, putting the timeline at 'a little more than a year', although he did not specify what type of nuclear device this estimate referred to.[120] Both estimates indicate that the bulk of Iran's time would be spent not on making the bomb itself, but on rendering it suitable for placing on a missile.

Much would depend on where Iran chose to produce the necessary HEU. It would take less time to do so at the Natanz site, because it bears the largest number of centrifuges. However, Natanz is more vulnerable to military attack, because its enrichment halls are buried only 8 metres underground (versus 91 metres at Fordow), and protected mostly by dirt (versus rock at Fordow).[121]

At Fordow, which might therefore be a preferable site for breakout, it would take between 9–15 weeks, or as little as 5–6 weeks if Iran slightly increases the number of centrifuges.[122] These estimates are highly sensitive to the number, type and efficiency of centrifuges at these facilities, and

[119] *CBS News*, 'The Defense Secretary: Leon Panetta', 29 January 2012.
[120] Dan De Luce, 'If Iran Builds Bomb, US Has a Year to Act: Panetta', *AFP*, 11 September 2012.
[121] 'Iran's Nuclear Matrix', *Washington Post*, 12 April 2012
[122] Albright and Walrond, 'Iranian Production of 19.75 Percent Enriched Uranium', p. 8.

therefore are marked by a considerable margin of error. However, Iran, as of November 2011, is still using its older IR-1 centrifuges rather than the newer versions with which it has experimented.[123] The figures here assume that Iran continues to struggle with making its newer centrifuges operational.

However, it is important to note that Iran faces a high risk of detection should it start reconfiguring centrifuges to enrich uranium beyond 20 per cent – something that has no plausible peaceful purpose (some Iranian officials have raised the idea of a nuclear submarine, which would require higher-enriched uranium, but this is fanciful).

The IAEA conducts regular inspections at Natanz and Fordow, including some on two hours' notice.[124] Given this, Iran would either have to conduct breakout 'in plain sight' – that is, while inspections were ongoing – and accept a high risk of detection, or expel inspectors (and dismantle the accompanying detection systems, like IAEA cameras) – an act that would be considered tantamount to breakout and would almost certainly be met with the use of force.

There is a further possibility: that Iran might choose not to conduct its breakout at a known facility, but instead break IAEA safeguards and send its partially enriched uranium to a (hypothetical) secret facility for the final leap to weapons-grade nuclear material. The time it would take to achieve breakout would then depend entirely on how many centrifuges were at this facility and how they were arranged. If such a secret site were on the scale of Fordow, the timeline would be similar – but concealing such a large plant would be difficult, especially as the diversion of uranium would be detected and an intense hunt would be underway.[125]

Even if Iran were to succeed in producing fissile material entirely covertly, or it expelled inspectors and left the international community in the dark, the United States and others are reported to believe that they would still have little trouble in detecting the crucial steps of weaponisation – by examining satellite evidence of conventional explosives detonation relevant to warhead design; intelligence from Iran's scientific community; and changes in the status of hitherto dormant facilities alleged to have led pre-2003 weaponisation research.[126]

Yet, assuming Iran succeeded in producing and then protecting the necessary fissile material, how long would it take to fabricate a bomb? The

---

[123]   Director General of the IAEA, GOV/2012/37, 'Implementation of the NPT Safeguards Agreement', p. 5.
[124]   Mark Hibbs, 'IAEA Inspectors' Risk in Iran', Arms Control Wonk blog, 20 August 2012.
[125]   See Michael A Levi, 'Limiting Iranian Nuclear Activities: Options and Consequences', Council on Foreign Relations Working Paper, February 2011, pp. 5–6.
[126]   David E Sanger, 'On Iran, Questions of Defense and Response Divide U.S. and Israel', *New York Times*, 6 March 2012.

timeline for this depends on how reliable such a device would need to be, whether it would need to be made deliverable by ballistic missile or merely serve as a technology demonstrator, and how much work Iran has already completed in secret.

In September 2012, it was alleged that 'new and significant intelligence' bolstered earlier findings that Iran had undertaken computer modelling of nuclear explosions in 2008 and 2009, while some sources allege that Iran continued these studies after 2009.[127] Such research would shorten the time between creating fissile material to producing a bomb. However, it is likely that warhead fabrication is at least as time-consuming as producing HEU, particularly when one takes into account the handicap of 'Iran's long-standing authoritarian management culture', a problem that has afflicted comparable nuclear programmes in other autocratic states, as comparative research by Jacques Hymans has indicated.[128]

Iran is undoubtedly shortening its breakout timeline. More MEU and more centrifuges mean that the timeline for fissile-material production is shrinking. Once Iran has enough MEU for the number of hypothetically desired bombs, the creation of more is no longer useful in further reducing this timeline. However, more centrifuges are useful, as they allow that fixed amount of MEU to be turned into fissile material more quickly.

Yet, regardless of these timelines, the greater problems for Iran are those of detection on the one hand and vulnerability to attack on the other. Each of the pathways to breakout carries great risks: Iran could expel inspectors and complicate detection, but it would remain just as vulnerable to having its facilities destroyed; alternatively, Iran could smuggle its MEU to a secret site, but such a diversion is guaranteed to be detected – and the site, if found, would also be subject to attack.

Unless it can be assumed that the likelihood of detection and vulnerability to attack are highly sensitive to breakout time – for instance, that it takes at least two months to find a secret site or move military forces into the region – then a shortened timeline does not, by itself, mitigate these basic constraints on breakout. Iran cannot, therefore, have a high degree of confidence in its ability to breakout without detection and subsequent attack.

Does Iran Want Nuclear Weapons?
Capability alone cannot tell us about intentions. A number of states can and do possess relatively short lead times and nevertheless refrain from building nuclear weapons. Japan, for instance, with huge stockpiles of

---

[127] Greg Thielmann and Kelsey Davenport, 'Clarifying the Record on Iran's Alleged Nuclear Weapons Program', *Arms Control Now*, 11 September 2012.
[128] Jacques E C Hymans, 'Botching the Bomb', *Foreign Affairs* (May/June 2012).

plutonium and advanced technology, would be no more than three to five years away from producing a nuclear bomb.[129] Possessing the option of acquiring the bomb, rather than actually doing so, has been called 'nuclear hedging',[130] and it represents a *via media* between abjuring nuclear power or key elements of the fuel cycle and actually building nuclear weapons. Certainly, Iran would gain prestige, and perhaps some deterrent value, from simply possessing the technical means – 'the art rather than the article', as Churchill put it in 1951.[131]

However, Iran cannot be compared to Japan. It is the pattern of persistent non-compliance with international agreements, prior military associations with the nuclear programme, and dubious rationales for certain types of nuclear activity that has led a large number of states to conclude that weaponisation, or the option of rapid weaponisation, is an important rationale for Iran's enrichment programme.

In December 2007, the Bush administration declassified part of its NIE on Iran, representing the consensus view of the country's intelligence community: 'we judge with high confidence that in fall 2003, Tehran halted its nuclear weapons program; we also assess with moderate-to-high confidence that Tehran at a minimum is keeping open the option to develop nuclear weapons'.[132] The NIE was reportedly clear that, prior to 2003, the Physics Research Center in Tehran – led by Mohsen Fakhrizadeh and renamed the Organization of Defensive Innovation and Research sometime in early 2011 – had indeed harboured a covert weapons programme which was later reconfigured for dual-use, but reversible, activities that continue today.[133] That programme was also documented in some detail in the IAEA's November 2011 report.[134]

The US has stuck to its judgment. In February 2011, the Director of National Intelligence James Clapper told Congress that 'we continue to assess Iran is keeping open the option to develop nuclear weapons', adding that 'we do not know, however, if Iran will eventually decide to

---

[129] Jeffrey Lewis, 'How Long For Japan To Build A Deterrent?', Arms Control Wonk blog, 28 December 2006; Jacques E C Hymans, 'Veto Players, Nuclear Energy, and Nonproliferation: Domestic Institutional Barriers to a Japanese Bomb',
International Security (Vol. 36, No. 2, Fall 2011), pp. 170, 186.
[130] Ariel E Levite, 'Never Say Never Again: Nuclear Reversal Revisited',
International Security (Vol. 27, No. 3, Winter 2002–03).
[131] Peter Hennessy (ed.), *Cabinets and the Bomb* (Oxford: Oxford University Press on behalf of the British Academy, 2007), p. 85.
[132] US National Intelligence Council, 'National Intelligence Estimate – Iran'.
[133] Jeffrey Lewis, 'The Ayatollah's Pregnant Pause', *Foreign Policy*, 15 August 2012.
[134] 'Annex: Possible Military Dimensions to Iran's Nuclear Programme', in Director General of the IAEA, 'Implementation of the NPT Safeguards Agreement and Relevant Provisions of Security Council Resolutions in the Islamic Republic of Iran', GOV/2011/65, 8 November 2011; note the highly detailed organisational chart on p. 5.

build nuclear weapons'. In April 2012, the chief of the Israeli army agreed, arguing that Iran 'is going step by step to the place where it will be able to decide whether to manufacture a nuclear bomb. It hasn't yet decided whether to go the extra mile ... I don't think [Khamenei] will want to go the extra mile'.[135]

Evidence of Iran's interest in weapons is based, in part, on non-public evidence of its prior weapons-related work, but there are several problems with the reliability and validity of this evidence. Much of it has been declared credible by the IAEA, which is an arm of the UN; however, critics point to a leaked US diplomatic cable in which the IAEA's director from 2009, Yukiya Amano, conceded that 'he was solidly in the US court on every key strategic decision, from high-level personnel appointments to the handling of Iran's alleged nuclear weapons program'.[136] This has given rise to concerns as to whether the IAEA is impartial in its judgments on Iran. One example that critics highlight is Amano's dissolution of the agency's office of external relations and policy co-ordination (Expo), a division that had previously been critical of assessments made by IAEA safeguards inspectors.[137]

Critics also cast doubt on the sourcing and reliability of the IAEA's evidence. In part, this is because member states – those with a political stake in the outcome – provide much of the evidence on which the IAEA draws. For example, Robert Kelley, a former IAEA inspector, has criticised the evidence in the IAEA's aforementioned November 2011 report, arguing that 'two of the three [pieces of evidence for Iranian nuclear weapons activity after 2003] are attributed only to two member states, so the sourcing is impossible to evaluate. In addition, their validity is called into question by the agency's handling of the third piece of evidence', pertaining to research into a neutron initiator. This, says Kelley, 'was earlier at the centre of what appeared to be a misinformation campaign' using a potentially fabricated document.[138] The problem of assessing evidence that has been provided by interested member states, and which is therefore prone to manipulation or fabrication, is fundamentally unresolvable, and can only be evaluated based on one's faith in the validation process and reliability of the IAEA and its staff.

However, criticism of Iran is also based on the characteristics of its enrichment programme, with Iran's critics making several points. First, the

---

[135] Amos Harel, 'IDF Chief to Haaretz: I Do Not Believe Iran Will Decide to Develop Nuclear Weapons', *Haaretz*, 25 April 2012.
[136] *Guardian*, 'US Embassy Cables: New UN Chief is "Director General of All States, but in Agreement with Us"', 2 December 2009.
[137] Julian Borger, 'Nuclear Watchdog Chief Accused of Pro-Western Bias over Iran', *Guardian*, 22 March 2012
[138] Robert Kelley, 'Nuclear Arms Charge Against Iran is No Slam Dunk: Robert Kelley', *Bloomberg*, 11 January 2012.

secrecy of Iran's programme, both in terms of procurement and construction, indicates its malign intentions. In this view, a clandestine programme signals a desire to breakout without detection, whereas a fully declared programme would preclude such covert breakout, and would therefore suggest (though not necessitate) peaceful intentions.

Second, critics argue that it is not cost-effective for Iran to enrich its own uranium unless it does so for at least ten reactors. The pattern of returns to scale with respect to enrichment is why, 'of the 30 countries with operational nuclear power plants, only one third produce their own uranium'.[139] Iran has in the past promised to build twenty nuclear power plants, although it has not committed the requisite resources.[140] At present, Iran's reactor plans amount to some new units at Bushehr, requests to Russia for two new reactors near Bushehr, and an indigenous reactor in western Iran – the construction of which is not scheduled to begin until 2014.[141] Although many other projects have been impeded for reasons beyond Iran's control, Iran is unlikely to hit the ten-reactor point within a reasonable timeframe to justify its uranium enrichment on the grounds of efficiency, let alone meet its even more ambitious targets. Moreover, Russia has promised to deliver all the required fuel to Bushehr, and to remove spent fuel rods, for a decade.[142] As for the medical isotopes which it is intended will be produced by the TRR, Iran could purchase these on the international market (as the US proposed in January 2010) or, at least, agree to swap its enriched uranium for fuel.[143]

Third, even if it wished to manufacture its own fuel plates, Iran now has sufficient MEU to operate the TRR for a decade. Enrichment is therefore occurring on a scale too large for medical isotopes alone but too small for fuelling the large array of envisioned reactors.

One often-misunderstood point is that Iran's plans for civil nuclear power are not contradicted by the fact of its hydrocarbon possessions. Oil- and gas-rich states, including others in the Gulf, often possess real or aspirational civil nuclear programmes, often assisted by Western states. However, there are other grounds on which to question the nuclear-energy rationale.

An academic study by the Los Alamos National Laboratory concluded that 'it is clear that Iran's nuclear program as now structured will not achieve this goal [of energy independence], and in fact may delay it by diverting capital and other resources from projects that would address

---

[139] Fitzpatrick, 'Containing the Iranian Nuclear Crisis', p. 75.

[140] David E Sanger and William J Broad, 'A Defiant Iran Vows to Build Nuclear Plants', *New York Times*, 29 November 2009.

[141] World Nuclear Association, 'Nuclear Power in Iran', 31 August 2012.

[142] Peter Crail, 'Bushehr Fuel Loading Commences', *Arms Control Today*, September 2010.

[143] Glenn Kessler, 'U.S. Unveils Offer to Help Iran Purchase Medical Isotopes', *Washington Post*, 10 February 2010.

pressing current energy sector problems and contribute to ultimate energy independence for Iran'.[144] Since the revolution, Iran has struggled to keep oil production above 3.5 million barrels per day (bpd), which is barely over a half of the daily production under the Shah, who oversaw the production of 6 million bpd in his final years. Sanctions, technology denial, isolation and low oil prices (especially between 1986 and 2000) have all played a part in this;[145] but so too has domestic neglect and low investment, which raises the question of whether nuclear power is a cost-effective allocation of resources.

The fourth criticism is that Iran's negotiating style is viewed as obstructionist and designed only to defer pressure and create space for further enrichment. If Iran had peaceful intentions, critics argue, it would accept a political settlement that fulfilled its energy needs and co-operate more fully with the IAEA.

Iran contests each of these points, although it has acknowledged lying about its nuclear activities.[146] It argues that the clandestine nature of its programme, and its insistence on stringent terms for any political settlement involving uranium export and fuel supply, is the result of the history of its coercion at the hands of foreign powers. In the past, Iran has been denied nuclear technology and resources in which it has made investments, most notably with respect to the Eurodif consortium. Furthermore, Iran also points to the way in which its legal and overt pursuit of nuclear technology in the 1990s was aggressively blocked or hindered by the US and other states.[147]

In a 2004 interview with the *Financial Times*, Ali Akbar Salehi, who had been Iran's representative to the IAEA during the previous year's EU-Iranian negotiations, argued that the reliability of any nuclear fuel supply was also in doubt: 'the Europeans have said they would assure us of the supply of nuclear fuel for the lifetime of the power plants, which run for 60 years, which is almost three generations. Who can believe such a guarantee? The world may change, we don't know what will happen, even the European Union may break up in three generations'.[148]

---

[144] Thomas W Wood, Matthew D Milazzo, Barbara A Reichmuth and Jeffrey Bedell, 'The Economics of Energy Independence for Iran', *Nonproliferation Review* (Vol. 14, No. 1, March 2007), p. 89.
[145] Roger Stern, 'The Iranian Petroleum Crisis and United States National Security', *Proceedings of the National Academy of Sciences* (Vol. 104, No. 1, 2 January 2007), p. 381.
[146] Rick Gladstone and Christine Hauser, 'Iran's Top Atomic Official Says Nation Issued False Nuclear Data to Fool Spies', *New York Times*, 20 September 2012.
[147] Rowhani, 'Beyond the Challenges Facing Iran and the IAEA', p. 32.
[148] See Director General of the IAEA, GOV/2012/37, 'Implementation of the NPT Safeguards Agreement', pp. 5, 13.

Iran further contends that its programme has been subject to a variety of tacit and explicit military threats (from those in the 1980s by Iraq to more recent Israeli and American signals), therefore necessitating its protection through secrecy and fortification. Another, albeit unarticulated, concern may be that transparency and openness about past transgressions would undermine Iran's present credibility, thereby leaving it vulnerable to further pressure and potentially inviting military action.

Iran also claims that indigenous nuclear technology is important to its modernisation. Some, like MIT researcher Geoffrey Forden, have argued that Iranian enrichment is important to the development of an indigenous nuclear medicine industry, and that the country would save money by avoiding wastage that occurs when imported isotopes used for medical purposes decay during shipment.[149] With regards to the plausibility of its stated nuclear-energy ambitions, Iran would not be the only state to have over-invested in civil nuclear power. Nor would it be the only state to pursue chronically delayed prestige projects of questionable economic worth for reasons of scientific nationalism and domestic politics.

In June 2012, Iran's deputy naval commander added another rationale for enrichment by announcing that Iran had taken 'preliminary steps' in the development and construction of a nuclear-powered submarine. The reactors for such submarines can require uranium enriched up to weapons-grade level, which in this case is exempt from IAEA safeguards and therefore vulnerable to diversion for the purposes of making nuclear weapons.[150] However, the timing of the announcement, the prohibitive technological and financial obstacles to designing and building such a submarine, and the littoral rather than blue-water nature of Iranian naval ambitions all suggest that this was little more than a pretext for higher-grade enrichment – either to serve as a bargaining chip in negotiations, or as a cover for enrichment beyond that required for the research reactor.

It is impossible to judge definitively the sincerity of both the accusations and the claims, although some Iranian claims – like the supposed ambition for a nuclear submarine – strain credulity. Iran could alleviate many of these concerns by fuller co-operation with the IAEA, something it has resisted on narrow legal grounds despite the enormous advantages it would reap from credibly demonstrating its peaceful intentions. Although Western officials remain intensely suspicious of Iran's rationale for enrichment, they tend to underestimate the degree to which the rest of the world – including the non-aligned states and rising

---

[149] Geoffrey Forden, 'A Primer on Iran's Medical Reactor Plans', Arms Control Wonk blog, 4 October 2009.
[150] Thomas Erdbrink and Rick Gladstone, 'Iran's President Says New Sanctions Are Toughest Yet', *New York Times*, 3 July 2012.

powers – are more sympathetic to Iran's narrative, and the importance to Iran of preserving some enrichment capability. Indeed, many of these states themselves want to retain the option of developing or expanding indigenous nuclear-power programmes, and have come to resent what they see as attempts by Western powers to deny them, and Iran in particular, this technology in a discriminatory fashion.[151]

The Drivers of the Iranian Nuclear Programme

Iran's nuclear programme and its alleged military dimensions are likely the result of four motivations: energy generation, scientific nationalism or prestige (including self-sufficiency[152]), a nuclear-weapons capability, and possession of nuclear weapons themselves. These motivations have been present to varying degrees throughout the last five decades of the existence of the Iranian nuclear programme.

The desire for weapons likely peaked in the period between the late 1980s and 2003 – ironically, a period in which pragmatic and then reformist tendencies were most prominent within Iran. As discussed earlier in this chapter, Iran's threat perceptions also evolved during that period. In the 1980s, the regional threat from Iraq was by far the single most important factor – even if outside powers contributed to Iran's isolation. In the 1990s, the enlarged US presence in the Middle East grew more prominent in Iranian strategic thinking. Yet just as the threat to Iran was perceived to be at its greatest (or perhaps because it was so), in the few years after 2001, with US forces on each side of Iran, Iran was judged to have paused its weapons programme.

2003 proved to be a pivotal moment. The US intelligence community believes that American pressure was instrumental in the pause. However, the demise of Saddam Hussein's Iraq also removed a major source of threat. It is impossible to assess the relative importance of the two in Iranian strategic thinking; yet both of these explanations are in fact compatible with a Realist interpretation of Iranian behaviour. In the 1980s and 1990s, Iran may have decided that its security was maximised by pursuing a nuclear-weapons programme but, after 2003, with growing

---

[151] See Diego Santos Vieira de Jesus, 'The Brazilian Way', *Nonproliferation Review* (Vol. 17, No. 3, October 2010); Sebnem Udum, 'Turkey's Nuclear Comeback: An Energy Renaissance in an Evolving Regional Security Context', *Nonproliferation Review* (Vol. 17, No. 2, July 2010); Jorge G Castaneda, 'Not Ready for Prime Time: Why Including Emerging Powers at the Helm Would Hurt Global Governance', *Foreign Affairs* (September/October 2010).

[152] Seyed Hossein Mousavian, in his list of 'major Iranian security objectives', places 'Iran with self-sufficiency on nuclear [and other] technology' at the very top, above even an end to the US presence in the region. See Mousavian, *The Iranian Nuclear Crisis*, p. 3.

international pressure and the threat of US invasion, it was maximised by reversing this policy. (However, it is important to note that external pressure is mediated through domestic politics, and different factions within Iran have interpreted pressure and security in different ways.)

It is therefore impossible to draw the simplistic conclusion that more pressure always elicits more concessions. 2003 was *sui generis*, because a notably hawkish US administration had invaded two countries, and was promulgating a highly activist international agenda. US threats against other states, including Iran, were uniquely credible. This was not just because of the trauma of the terrorist attacks of 9/11, and the way in which that trauma legitimated actions that would earlier have been unacceptable (and would later become so again). It was also because large numbers of US forces were located in theatre, on the other side of two of Iran's borders. Moreover, the rapid military successes against Iraq and Afghanistan served as plainly visible demonstrations that the American use of force against weaker states was both highly effective and apparently low-cost.

Only when insurgencies developed in both of those countries, producing strategic defeats in each case, did that threat lose credibility. This was certainly the interpretation of Hassan Rowhani, Iran's then-most senior nuclear negotiator, who noted in 2005 that 'if our case had been sent to the Security Council [in October 2003], the Americans even would have allowed themselves to consider a military attack. But as of today, I am sure that military attack is not an option anymore'.[153]

After the costly and politically sensitive military campaigns of the past decade, no US administration can credibly threaten a manpower-intensive invasion and occupation of Iran of the kind that would be necessary to halt and monitor all Iranian nuclear activities in the long term. The American departure from Iraq and likely withdrawal of combat troops from Afghanistan in 2014 mean that it will not be able to replicate the operational posture of 2001–03 that rendered its implicit military threat against Iran credible. Air strikes, without some element of ground support, do not pose a similar threat because they are unlikely to have the same regime-destroying effect as a full-scale invasion, and may even consolidate domestic support for the regime.

Iran's domestic politics has also transformed over the past decade. Iran's tactical co-operation with the US in Afghanistan and the suspension of its nuclear programme both occurred when Iranian reformists formally held power in Tehran. They were predisposed towards better relations with the international community, and may have perceived greater opportunities for co-operation than the more hard-line factions that

---

[153] Mehdi Mohammadi, 'Interview with Dr Hasan Rowhani', trans. FBIS, *Keyhan*, 2005, p. 8, <http://www.armscontrolwonk.com/file_download/99/Rowhani_Interview.pdf>, accessed 19 October 2012.

dominate today. This does not mean reformists were 'anti-nuclear'. As we have seen, reformists like Mir Hossein Mousavi have been public and vocal opponents of nuclear concessions. Nor was the reformist leadership driving nuclear policy in 2003 (that prerogative was and is Khamenei's). Nevertheless, it is reasonable to suggest that the government, as a whole, was more amenable to co-operation with the West in 2003 than it would later become.

As Ray Takeyh argues, 'the reason why Iran embarked on a judicious recalibration of its interests in both episodes stemmed not just from pressures, but also from the presence of a powerful, pragmatic coalition within the government that managed to prevail in internal deliberations'.[154] Iranian restraint persisted even as American forces were increasingly bogged down in Iraq, suggesting that domestic political conditions – and not just external threat – were important. (However, the possibility that the removal of the Iraqi threat by the US in 2003 was also a contributing factor to this posture of restraint must be considered.) In contrast, the present Iranian government believes that 'even merely suspending the programme will challenge the legitimacy of the state'.[155] Yet the Iranian government of 2003 did *not* hold this belief. It publicly suspended a core part of the nuclear programme (enrichment activity) and adhered to that suspension for years. The application of pressure today will not therefore function as it did in 2003.

A 'Goldilocks Theory' of Pressure?

Threats have curtailed Iran's programme – but they have also spurred it on, as in the 1980s: therefore, there may be a non-linear relationship between threats and Iran's nuclear choices. Many of those who cite the 2007 NIE as evidence that Iran had paused its nuclear programme disregard the other conclusion of that report – that pressure and scrutiny were instrumental in persuading Iran to take that step. Too little pressure, and Iran may see no reason to abide by its international obligations. Too much, however – particularly in the absence of attractive and credible inducements – and Iranian elites may come to place a much higher value on a nuclear-weapons capability (the status quo) or nuclear weapons themselves.

Sceptics might ask why, if this is so, the military threat in 2003 did not also lead to Iran accelerating rather than pausing its nuclear weapons activities. One explanation is that the threat was uniquely immediate, regime-threatening and coincident with a pragmatic coalition within the Iranian government and the shattering of Iraq, Iran's primary regional rival. Some will find this explanation unsatisfying. To some extent, it amounts to a 'Goldilocks theory' of pressure, whereby too little and too much pressure

---

[154] Ray Takeyh, 'Iran's Missing Moderates', *New York Times*, 18 March 2012.
[155] Takeyh and Maloney, 'The Self-Limiting Success of Iran Sanctions', p. 12.

both produce bad outcomes. However, the history of Iran's nuclear programme suggests that the ever-increasing application of pressure may not be a fruitful strategy. Chapter III of this study, on current policy, applies these principles to the sanctions effort presently underway.

Coda: The Arab Spring

How has the Arab Spring – the wave of political mobilisation across the Arab world during 2011 and 2012 – affected Iran and its nuclear ambitions?

Iran's regional outlook has been traditionally conditioned by its own self-image as a regional hegemon; its deep antipathy towards Iraq during Sunni rule in Baghdad; longstanding rivalries with Sunni Arab powers in the Gulf; its hostility towards the US, itself an ally and protector of those powers; its rivalry with Israel, particularly pronounced from the mid-1990s onwards; and, finally, its alliances with Levantine powers, notably Syria, and non-state armed groups.

Iranian hostility to Arab powers has a strategic aspect that predates its revolution. The day before Britain ended its security responsibilities in the Gulf in 1971, Iran – under the Shah – seized three islands from the United Arab Emirates in a dispute that remains active. Nonetheless, a regional security system evolved from 1971 to 1978, as part of which each major power in the region broadly accepted the status quo.[156] That system was fractured by the Iranian revolution, 'a pivot of modern Middle Eastern history'.[157] Iranian agents were blamed for plots to destabilise Bahrain in 1981, Saudi Arabia in 1984 and Kuwait in 1985.[158]

Although the smaller Gulf Arab states – like Qatar and Oman – continued to maintain relatively strong ties with Iran, both to hedge against Saudi Arabian power and for other reasons (Oman was grateful for Iranian counter-insurgency assistance), an Arab coalition against Iran eventually did coalesce, with the Gulf Cooperation Council (GCC) formed in 1981, and Arab states providing material support to Saddam Hussein in his war against Iran between 1980 and 1988. Although the Iraqi invasion of Kuwait later split this Arab coalition, and diverted some Arab attention towards Baghdad rather than Tehran, this period also saw a change in the American posture. From 1991, the US joined the balancing effort, targeting both Iran and Iraq, by forward deploying its own forces and selling arms to regional allies wary of both of these states. Between the

---

[156] Gause, *The International Relations of the Persian Gulf*, p. 43.
[157] *Ibid.*, p. 45.
[158] Kristian Coates Ulrichsen, *Insecure Gulf: The End of Certainty and the Transition to the Post-Oil Era* (New York: Columbia University Press, 2011), pp. 39, 55.

two periods 1991–94 and 1993–96, the Middle East grew as a proportion of US arms sales from 63.45 per cent to 76.1 per cent.[159]

Iranian-Arab enmity is and has been strategic in nature, but it also has sectarian and ethno-linguistic dimensions. Iran is a mostly Shia Persian state, whereas the Gulf powers are predominantly Sunni Arab states. Moreover, many Shia communities in the Arab world are socially, economically and politically marginalised. This chimes with Shia Islam's historic perception of itself as oppressed in historical, theological and political terms.[160] In both Iraq and Bahrain, Sunni minority regimes ruled over Shia majorities, and Shia minorities in Saudi Arabia and elsewhere remained downtrodden. Revolutionary Iran was therefore a triple threat: first, because it aspired to Islamic leadership across sectarian boundaries, with an offer of a clerical model (*velayat-e-faqih*, or rule by Islamic jurists); second, because that model was a direct threat to the Saudi ideal; and third, because it held particular appeal to Shia communities.[161]

A leaked 1985 diplomatic cable from the US embassy in Cairo describes some of these fears. It notes that the Saudi Arabian leadership 'recognise[s] the fundamental, theological hostility of the Iranian regime and understand[s] that until the [Iranian] revolution has been blunted and its nature significantly transformed, it will represent a threat to the Al Saud [rule in Saudi Arabia]'. However, the same cable notes the Saudi perception that 'the likelihood of Iranian-inspired subversion in Saudi Arabia is now small, and that the danger of [Iranian] subversion in other Gulf countries is probably containable'. Moreover, the Saudi leadership is 'acutely aware, too, of the long-term need for a decent working relationship with Iran [based on] shared interests'.[162]

A better working relationship did indeed evolve during the 1990s (though this period was not without major setbacks), and particularly after the election of a reformist Iranian president in 1997, but this period of détente did not prove durable. Saudi and Arab fears heightened after 2001, when the narrative of a 'Shia crescent' began to take shape. This putative axis of Shia power was said to run from Iran to Iraq to Saudi Arabia's Shia-dominated, oil-rich Eastern Province, and thence to Lebanon and Syria. Sunni governments fell in Iraq and Afghanistan, empowering forces

[159] Anthony H Cordesman, 'World Arms Sales and The Middle East: Changing Trends in Economic Impact, Purchases by Country, New Agreements, Deliveries, and Suppliers', Center for Strategic and International Studies, October 1997, p. 59.
[160] Michael Axworthy, *Iran: Empire of the Mind: A History from Zoroaster to the Present Day* (London: Penguin, 2008), pp. 124–25.
[161] F Gregory Gause, *Oil Monarchies: Domestic and Security Challenges in the Arab Gulf States* (New York: Council on Foreign Relations, 1994), pp. 31–33.
[162] Roscoe S Suddarth, 'US Embassy Cable: Saudi Policy Toward Iran', US embassy, Riyadh, 12 June 1985, <http://cables.mrkva.eu/cable.php?id=67>, accessed 19 October 2012.

that were, at the very least, less hostile to Iran than their predecessors. In Lebanon, Hizbullah assumed a prominent role in the state.

At their crudest, these fears portray Shia groups everywhere as Iranian fifth columnists, eager to impose radical theocratic rule and Iran's geopolitical preferences. However, as Kristian Coates Ulrichsen observes, these theories 'rest on a flawed ascription of pan-Shiite transnational loyalties and an ascription of monolithic unity within Shiism that does not exist in reality'.[163]

Israel, for its part, perceives a threat from both Sunni and Shia powers (Hamas and Hizbullah respectively), and therefore sees the Iranian threat in somewhat different terms. Unlike Saudi Arabia, Israel is not concerned about Iranian political subversion. However, the resilience of Iranian allies – like Hizbullah in its war with Israel in 2006 – and the belligerent anti-Israel rhetoric of the Ahmadinejad government after 2005 heightened Israeli concerns.

Post 2011

The Arab Spring has had an uneven effect on these rivalries. Iran's influence has risen in some places and fallen in others. In other places, anti-Iran coalitions have fractured, without necessarily resulting in greater Iranian influence.

The first and most significant shift was the fall of Egyptian President Hosni Mubarak. His demise empowered long-suppressed Islamist groups there, notably the Muslim Brotherhood, and engendered greater popular pressures on Egyptian foreign policy. Mubarak was an ally of Saudi Arabia and sceptical of Iranian intentions; but while there remain strong anti-Iranian sentiments in Cairo, it is likely that a more democratic Egypt will be more open to dialogue and accommodation and with Tehran. (Egyptian-Iranian relations are explored in greater depth in Chapter IV of this study, which examines potential nuclear proliferation beyond Iran.)

Democratisation in Egypt also presents severe challenges for Israel. The 1979 Camp David peace treaty between Israel and Egypt has been crucial to Israel's defence posture, by mitigating the threat from its southern flank. The army may, as in Pakistan, dominate foreign policy in the emerging Egyptian system; but if Egypt were to seek to re-negotiate or repudiate the treaty, this would put considerable pressure on Israel, particularly at a time when Turkey and Israel, once allies, are growing estranged. Such changes would be welcomed in Tehran; yet this outcome would not necessarily enhance Iran's influence, and it might even mean that Iran would cede some influence over Palestinian militant and political groups to Cairo.

---

[163] Ulrichsen, *Insecure Gulf*, p. 52.

The Arab Spring's second geopolitical impact is on Saudi Arabia. Riyadh and allied Gulf states have reacted to the calls for democracy sweeping across North Africa and the Middle East with alarm. They fear not just contagion, but also that popular mobilisation will benefit pro-Iran factions. Indeed, they see Iranian interference as lying behind much of the region's unrest.

The Saudi Arabian response to regional protests was swift and powerful.[164] As Toby Jones explains, Riyadh 'mobilized both its tremendous wealth and its capacity for violence to crush democratic insurgencies at home and around the region'.[165] Although Saudi Arabia supported popular movements both in Libya, where Colonel Qadhafi's regime had long become estranged from the Arab world, and in Iran's ally Syria, it also led a pan-Arab force into Bahrain to crush the revolt there.

Saudi Arabia also sees itself combating Iranian influence in northern Yemen, where Iran reportedly abets the northern Houthi rebel movement, abutting Saudi Arabian territory; in Lebanon, where Iran-backed Hizbullah has supplanted pro-Saudi Sunni factions over the past five years; in Iraq, where Saudi Arabia has begun to re-engage with the Al-Maliki government in 2012, after years of neglect; in Syria, where Saudi Arabian officials have committed to arming the opposition to Bashar Al-Assad, who in turn receives Iranian assistance; and elsewhere. Accordingly, Riyadh has sought to increase regional solidarity amongst like-minded states, under its leadership. In 2011, it invited the non-Gulf monarchies of Jordan and Morocco to join the GCC, and in 2012 attempted, largely unsuccessfully, to form a Gulf Union that would enhance collective security.

Despite its efforts, Saudi Arabia has not succeeded in permanently subduing popular pressures. In fact, Saudi-sponsored sectarianism has likely worsened some of these problems over the longer term. Moreover, predominantly Shia protests in the country's own Eastern Province continue apace.

Early in the Arab Spring, Iran had indeed sought to characterise the incipient uprisings as Islamic revolutions following the model of 1979. This narrative found little traction anywhere:[166] even amongst the predominantly Shia protesters of Bahrain – who, like Shia elsewhere, have some theological ties to the clerical establishment within Iran and to individual clerics – there was negligible appetite for political direction from abroad *or* the adoption of an Iranian political model. Influential parts of the Bahraini opposition have

---

[164] Mehran Kamrava, 'The Arab Spring and the Saudi-Led Counterrevolution', *Orbis* (Vol. 56, No. 1, Winter 2012).

[165] Toby Craig Jones, 'Saudi Arabia Versus the Arab Spring', *Raritan: A Quarterly Review* (Vol. 31, No. 2, 2011), p. 58.

[166] Robert F Worth, 'Effort to Rebrand Arab Spring Backfires in Iran', *New York Times*, 2 February 2012.

called for judicial reform, the separation of powers and efforts to curb discrimination rather than theocratic governance.[167] Moreover, an independent report commissioned by the Bahraini regime itself found no evidence to warrant the charge of Iranian interference inside Bahrain.[168]

This does not mean that democratic shifts within Bahrain or elsewhere in the Gulf would leave the strategic balance unchanged. The Sunni-dominated status quo enables the basing of US forces in Bahrain, for instance, which in turn functions as an 'overwatch' force in the region and a deterrent against any Iranian aggression. The US could engage in 'offshore balancing', and project power without such regional bases, but it would be a far more demanding task, entailing longer lead times for military action.

The US has reacted to the Arab Spring in a conservative fashion, and with a focus on counteracting any perceived expansion in Iranian influence. Although it did not actively seek to prop up the Mubarak regime – an ally – it has refrained from applying heavy pressure to Bahrain, Saudi Arabia or other autocratic allies to engage in reform. In late December 2011, Washington agreed an arms package worth $30 billion for Saudi Arabia.[169] It also agreed an $11 billion-package for Iraq, despite (or even because of) fears of Iraq's tilt towards Iran, and in May 2012 resumed arms sales to Bahrain.

These measures are all seen as efforts to preserve the substantial military edge of the anti-Iran bloc, and are intended to signal that any perceived political vulnerabilities in the pro-US Arab states will not be allowed to become opportunities for Iranian subversion.

No-one 'Won' the Arab Spring

Overall, the conclusion that Iran has 'won' the Arab Spring should be strongly resisted. Such conclusions usually acquiesce in the dominant assumptions of Arab political elites that regional shifts are always zero-sum. In this view, the weakening of Arab states and of anti-Iran actors automatically represents an Iranian victory.[170]

---

[167] Toby C Jones, 'Bahrain's Revolutionaries Speak: An Exclusive Interview with Bahrain's Coalition of February 14th Youth', *Jadaliyya*, 22 March 2012.

[168] Mahmoud Cherif Bassiouni, Nigel Rodley, Badria Al-Awadhi, Philippe Kirsch and Mahnoush H Arsanjani, 'Report of the Bahrain Independent Commission of Inquiry', Bahrain Independent Commission of Inquiry, 23 November 2011, pp. 383–85.

[169] Mark Landler and Steven Lee Myers, 'With $30 Billion Arms Deal, U.S. Bolsters Saudi Ties', *New York Times*, 29 December 2011.

[170] Along these lines, James Dobbins notes that the 'Saudi leadership appears to perceive that any loosening of the status quo will result in a net gain for Iran – an exaggerated perception of threat that plays into the hands of the Islamic Republic and puts Riyadh at odds with Washington's attempts to encourage measured and peaceful reform in the region'. See Dobbins, Nader, Kaye and Wehrey, *Coping with a Nuclearizing Iran*, p. 33.

In some cases, this may be true. The fall of Saddam Hussein certainly increased Iranian influence, if not by as much as is sometimes assumed. However, this is not necessarily true elsewhere. In many cases, democratic trends *will* make it harder to fashion what are seen as anti-Iran policies. For instance, Kuwait's parliament – with better Shia representation than elsewhere, thanks to its greater degree of representation – resisted sending forces to Bahrain as part of the GCC force.

The democratic trend in the Arab world is undoubtedly partial and reversible.[171] Nevertheless, popular pressure does increasingly exert itself on foreign policy in some Arab states, and this might have implications for policies towards Iran. A recent survey by the Arab Center for Research and Policy Studies demonstrated that, in contrast to *elite* Arab opinion, the vast majority of the Arab public does not believe that Iran poses a threat to the 'security of the Arab homeland'. Just 5 per cent of respondents named Iran as a source of threat, in contrast with 22 per cent and 51 per cent who named the US and Israel as threats, respectively.

The largest percentage viewing Iran as a threat was reported in Lebanon and Jordan (10 per cent), and the lowest (1 per cent or less) was reported in Egypt, Tunisia, Algeria, Mauritania and Sudan – with two of these, Egypt and Tunisia, being states that are likely to undergo more populist shifts in foreign policy, and therefore on their policies towards Iran. In Saudi Arabia, the state whose leadership is perhaps most fearful of Iran and most active in responding to the perceived threat posed by it, only 8 per cent believed that Iran presents a threat, far lower than that the 13 per cent who viewed the US as a threat.[172] These are strikingly low numbers.

Taken together, it is clear that popular Arab opinion is far less hostile to Iran than elite Arab opinion. *Ceteris paribus*, democratic pressures on policy are likely to result in less-hostile foreign policies towards Iran. However, in the actual democratic movements that together constitute those pressures, namely, the 'Arab Spring' as a series of concrete protest movements, revolutions and rebellions, 'Iran was irrelevant'.[173] Simply put, the Iranian political model did not motivate democratic activists, and Iranian influence was non-existent or negligible.

---

[171] Shashank Joshi, 'Reflections on the Arab Revolutions: Order, Democracy and Western Policy', *RUSI Journal* (Vol. 156, No. 2, April/May 2011).

[172] Arab Center for Research and Policy Studies, 'The Arab Opinion Project: The Arab Opinion Index', March 2012.

[173] Ali Ansari, Shahram Chubin and Hassan Hakimian, 'The Challenge of Uncertainty: Iran's Ambitions and Choices', transcript of panel discussion, Chatham House, London, 29 March 2012, p. 6.

This could change. If reform fails to accommodate Shia minorities, it is plausible that radicalisation and greater Iranian influence over disaffected communities may be observed in the future.[174] In the short term, however, a concerted Saudi-led counter-revolutionary effort, intensified American assistance to Gulf States, and Iran's own intensifying political and economic dysfunction means that the Sunni Arab political order, centred on Riyadh and underwritten by Washington, remains fundamentally resistant to Iranian ambitions, both real and contrived.

It is also important to recognise that the Arab Spring has generated opportunities for Iran's rivals, as well. The most consequential shift has taken place in Syria, where a peaceful protest movement evolved into an armed insurgency over the course of 2011 and 2012.

Iran and the Syrian Crisis

Syria is a crucially important state to Iran, despite the awkward marriage 'between secular Ba'athists and revolutionary Islamists', initially joined by their shared hostility towards Saddam Hussein's Iraq.[175] During the Iran-Iraq War, Syria proffered major intelligence and military support to Tehran, and gave the Iranian cause a much-needed Arab veneer. The two states have been bound closer both by a theological affinity (Syria's ruling dynasty is Alawite, a syncretic offshoot of Shia Islam) and, even during the Shah's reign, a shared interest in the Lebanese Shia community and Palestinian militant groups.[176]

Each state has drawn on the resources and advantages of the other. Despite Iran's independent channels of influence into Lebanon, 'Syria benefited from proximity and control of a major land border with [its neighbour], giving it the power to impede Iran's direct contacts with and provision of supplies' to Hizbullah.[177] Moreover, Hamas' leadership was expelled from Jordan in 1999 and has been based in the Syrian capital, Damascus, since then.[178]

---

[174] Shashank Joshi, 'The Middle East: The Persian Illusion', *World Today* (Vol. 67, No. 5, June 2011).

[175] Christopher Phillips, 'Syria and Iran: Diplomatic Alliance and Power in the Middle East', *British Journal of Middle Eastern Studies* (Vol. 38, No. 3, 2011).

[176] Hussein J Agha and Ahmad Samih Khalidi, *Syria and Iran: Rivalry and Cooperation* (New York: Royal Institute of International Affairs, 1995), pp. 1–8.

[177] Abbas William Samii, 'A Stable Structure on Shifting Sands: Assessing the Hizbullah-Iran-Syria Relationship', *Middle East Journal* (Vol. 62, No. 1, Winter 2008), pp. 37–38.

[178] Matthew Levitt, *Hamas: Politics, Charity, And Terrorism in the Service of Jihad* (New Haven, CT: Yale University Press, 2006), p. 45.

Iran has responded to Syria's uprising by allegedly providing manpower, intelligence, arms and funding to the Assad regime.[179] In September 2012, the commander of the IRGC confirmed that his forces were present in Syria, offering 'intellectual and advisory help'.[180] Several risks to Iran would stem from Assad's defeat, an outcome that looks increasingly likely after the wave of defections and assassinations from the summer of 2012, the rebel penetration of hitherto sanctuary areas such as Damascus, and the growing swathes of northern Syria slipping out of the regime's hands.

First, Iran would 'lose' its only real foothold in the Arab world, although perhaps only in a limited sense. Indeed, Burhan Ghalioun, former head of the Syrian National Council (now subsumed into a broader coalition), has explained that 'the current relationship between Syria and Iran is abnormal. There will be no special relationship with Iran. Breaking the exceptional relationship means breaking the strategic military alliance'.[181]

It is important to note that losing this foothold would *not* necessarily mean losing access either to Lebanon or Palestinian groups (Iran would retain independent channels). However, it would make that access somewhat harder. Moreover, Iran's allies could themselves become weaker. Hizbullah could lose supply lines and room for manoeuvre if Assad were to fall. That would reduce Iran's ability to use Hizbullah as leverage against Israel.

Second, the uprising in Syria is a wedge issue, driving Iran apart from allies and partners. It has already complicated Iran's relationship with both Hamas and Turkey.[182] Hamas clashed with the Assad regime when it refused to mount pro-government rallies and in February 2012, Hamas leader Ismail Haniyeh, speaking in Cairo, said, 'I salute all the nations of the Arab Spring and I salute the heroic people of Syria who are striving for freedom, democracy and reform'.[183] This was widely interpreted as a major breach with Syria. Furthermore, by late January, there were no Hamas leaders left in Damascus;[184] clearly, although the group did not announce the closure of its bureau there, it had all but abandoned Syria as a base.[185]

---

[179] Khaled Yacoub Oweis and Angus MacSwan, 'Iranian Ships Reach Syria, Assad Allies Show Support', *Reuters*, 20 February 2012; Joby Warrick and Liz Sly, 'U.S. Officials: Iran is Stepping up Lethal Aid to Syria', *Washington Post*, 4 March 2012.
[180] Ian Black, 'Iran Confirms it Has Forces in Syria and Will Take Military Action if Pushed', *Guardian*, 16 September 2012.
[181] Emile Hokayem, 'Syria and its Neighbours', *Survival* (Vol. 54, No. 2, April–May 2012), p. 8.
[182] On strained Turkish-Iranian ties, see ICG, 'In Heavy Waters', p. 21.
[183] Omar Fahmy and Nidal Al-Mughrabi, 'Hamas Ditches Assad, Backs Syrian Revolt', *Reuters*, 24 February 2012.
[184] Fares Akram, 'Hamas Leader Abandons Longtime Base in Damascus', *New York Times*, 27 January 2012.
[185] *Haaretz*, 'Final Member of Damascus-Based Hamas Politburo Leaves Syria', 5 February 2012.

This estrangement between Hamas and Syria is problematic for Iran. In mid-2011, while the Syrian uprising was at an early stage, Iran curtailed its funding for Hamas to coerce the group into supporting the Syrian regime.[186] Then, in March 2012, senior Hamas figures insisted that they would not participate in any war against Israel that might result from a military strike on Iranian nuclear facilities.[187] The dilemma for Iran is that it cannot pursue its interests in the Palestinian territories without some acknowledgement of Syria's interests there, but nor can it afford to abandon Hamas without breaking what it sees as 'a source of leverage over Israel and the broader peace process'. Either way, a key node in what Iran sees as an 'axis of resistance' (to Israeli, American and broader Western influence) is being placed under severe strain by the anti-government movement in Syria. Over time, this could cause greater splits within Hamas as Iran and Syria align with different factions, something that has repeatedly occurred in the past.

Moreover, Iran's material and military support of Syria is a distraction, diverting IRGC operatives from elsewhere. It will eventually become a burden on Iranian finances, particularly as the sanctions bite further.[188]

The Arab Spring and Iran's Nuclear Choices

How will these changes affect Tehran's calculus over its nuclear programme? There are a number of possible interpretations.

One set of arguments presumes that Iran perceives democratic movements to have weakened the US-backed Sunni Arab bloc, particularly in countries where Shia movements are challenging the status quo. Following on from the expansion of its influence in Lebanon, Iraq and Afghanistan over the past decade, Iran's aspirations for regional leadership have grown.

From this perspective, the events of 2011 have only exacerbated that trend. That might mean that Iran's leaders see themselves as negotiating from a position of strength, and will therefore be more inclined to make fewer concessions over, say, the issue of enrichment. It might also mean that factions within Iran favouring the development of nuclear weapons see this as an opportune period in which to do so.

The second point of view is that the potential loss of Iran's position in Syria would leave Tehran shorn of its most important diplomatic assets, and therefore licking its wounds. Efraim Halevy, a former Israeli national security adviser and ambassador, and director of Mossad from 1998 to

---

[186] *Haaretz*, 'Iran Cuts Hamas Funding for Failing to Show Support for Assad', 21 August 2011.
[187] Harriet Sherwood, 'Hamas Rules Out Military Support for Iran in any War with Israel', *Guardian*, 6 March 2012.
[188] Hokayem, 'Syria and its Neighbours', p. 9.

2002, has argued that 'ensuring ... Iran is evicted from its regional hub in Damascus would ... visibly dent its domestic and international prestige, possibly forcing a hemorrhaging regime in Tehran to suspend its nuclear policies'.[189] In a similar vein, in May 2012, diplomatic observers were 'struck by how deeply the crisis in Syria, Iran's most important regional ally, is affecting confidence in Tehran'.[190]

Should Iran decide that it is overstretched, it may consider its security to be best served by tactical conciliation in relation to the nuclear programme – an interpretation that is, perhaps, strengthened by Iran's efforts to include Syria on the agenda at nuclear talks. This may be a particularly likely outcome if Iran's retaliatory options to any military strike on its nuclear facilities, through Hizbullah and Hamas, are unreliable or weakening as a result of events in Syria.

However, a third, more realistic and less sanguine perspective is that the loss or estrangement of Iran's non-state armed allies would leave Iran less secure, more vulnerable and therefore more intent, in the final instance, on seeking a nuclear-weapons capability in order to offset the losses in its unconventional strength.

Indeed, the regional threat faced by Iran has never been just a symmetric and military one; instead it is an asymmetric and ideological or subversive threat. Iran's alliance with Palestinian, Lebanese and other militant groups has been a source of political influence and prestige. With the conventional military strength of the Gulf Arab powers growing (an illustration of comparative spending is given in Figure 2 in Chapter IV), and the US commitment to the region unshaken, it is possible, although by no means certain, that the trauma of regime change in Syria would bolster pro-nuclear voices in Iran.

It is impossible to judge with certainty whether a weaker or stronger Iran is more or less likely to view nuclear weapons, or a more advanced nuclear-weapons capability, in favourable terms; this is analogous to the problem of evaluating whether pressure is more or less likely to compel concessions, and Iranian decision-makers may be as divided on this question as they are on others. What should be recognised is that the relationship between Iran's strength and ambitions and its nuclear aspirations is likely to be complex and non-linear. In particular, sensitivity is needed to the danger that a significantly weaker Iran might perceive itself as more vulnerable, and might therefore be more likely to feel the need to push its nuclear capabilities further.

---

[189] Efraim Halevy, 'Iran's Achilles' Heel', *New York Times*, 7 February 2012.
[190] Julian Borger, 'Hopes Grow of a Confidence-Building Deal on Iranian Nuclear Programme', *Guardian*, 16 May 2012.

III. POLICY TODAY

Iran and the West are currently locked in a prolonged stand-off that each sees in zero-sum terms. The official Western position is that any Iranian enrichment programme is unacceptable: not only out of concern for upholding existing UN Security Council resolutions, but also because of the way in which such a programme would take Iran closer to having enough fissile material for a nuclear bomb. As such, the West has two primary demands: first, that Iran cease or limit its enrichment programme; and second, that Iran settle its outstanding issues with the IAEA concerning alleged past and present work on nuclear weapons.

For Iran, however, the right to enrich uranium is an integral part of its rights under the NPT to use nuclear technology for peaceful purposes. Given this, Iran has two primary demands of its own: that it be allowed to maintain an enrichment programme, and that the apparatus of pressure – principally, sanctions – be removed or weakened.[1]

These two sets of demands, in their maximalist forms, are mutually incompatible. Iran wants to enrich, and the West does not want it to do so. This incompatibility has produced a stalemate.

Although both sides have indicated a willingness to abandon elements of their respective core positions, these indications have been oblique and usually stated through easily deniable channels. Meanwhile, the most recent series of formal negotiations, held during 2012 in Istanbul, Baghdad and Moscow, has failed to yield any compromises.

In the most recent talks, in Moscow in June 2012, Western demands centred on a proposal known as 'stop, shut, ship', whereby Iran would stop what was seen as its most dangerous enrichment of uranium, to 20 per cent, would export its existing stocks of that material abroad, and would altogether shut its Fordow facility – all in exchange for nuclear fuel and much-needed aircraft parts. On the one hand, this proposal was more favourable to Iran than the Geneva talks of 2009, discussed in Chapter II. After all, it would have allowed Iran to continue producing and to maintain

---

[1] A third demand, that Iran cease work on the potentially plutonium-producing Arak reactor, has received less attention in diplomatic talks and is therefore not dealt with here. However, it will become a much more significant issue in 2013.

its existing stocks of LEU. However, on the other hand, it did not address either of Iran's core demands.

Some have previously argued that Iran would be open to sacrificing its higher-grade enrichment if it received, in exchange, sanctions relief (although not the removal of sanctions in their entirety) from, for instance, EU restrictions on insurance for Iranian oil tankers. The P5 + 1 did not offer or suggest sanctions relief as a point of concession, and did not therefore test Iran's willingness for any such compromise. This was in contrast to earlier suggestions, likely emanating from P5 + 1 sources, that the West *did* consider sanctions relief to be an acceptable counterweight for Iranian suspension of higher-grade enrichment, which would thereby result in 'a deal that limits enrichment while preserving the right to enrich'.[2] Iran, for its part, did not suggest such a compromise itself, and in fact re-interpreted certain Western concessions – such as the provision of fuel – as *Iranian* concessions, complicating the entire process and increasing frustration with the Iranian negotiators.

Why did the West fail to offer sanctions relief to Iran, and why did Iran fail to suggest any such compromise itself? The underlying reasons for each side's maintenance of a maximalist position are important – particularly as compromise remains the most probable way out of the impasse.

Western policy assumes that Iran is ill-prepared to bear the consequences of a long-term stand-off while it remains under an unprecedentedly severe sanctions regime and faces ongoing efforts to retard the enrichment programme. Over time, it is argued, Iran will be forced to acquiesce to a suspension of at least major parts of its enrichment programme, notably the higher-grade enrichment at the Fordow facility, and to co-operate with the IAEA in good faith, lest economic strangulation threaten the survival of the regime itself. As such, there is perceived to be little incentive to offer sanctions relief when the perpetuation of those sanctions is presumed to create a weaker Iran, and therefore a stronger Western bargaining position, in the future.

Additionally, Western policy-makers have intensified pressure on Iran in great measure out of fear that Israel will launch a premature or counterproductive military strike against Iranian nuclear facilities. Indeed, many Western officials acknowledge that sanctions are seen less as productive sources of pressure on Iran and more as a means of assuaging Israel.[3]

Iran, by contrast, judges that it can withstand this pressure into the longer term, and that its creation of new 'facts on the ground' – and therefore of new areas of bargaining leverage – has allowed it to protect

---

[2] David Ignatius, 'The Stage is Set For a Deal with Iran', *Washington Post*, 18 April 2012.
[3] Author interviews with diplomats from multiple P5 + 1 states, London, May–August 2012.

the core of its enrichment programme. Whereas the focus of negotiations in 2009 was on LEU, it is now on higher-grade enrichment, thereby insulating the lower-grade activity from as much attention and censure. Moreover, the status quo allows Iran to accumulate enriched uranium and shorten its hypothetical breakout time, creating greater pressure on the West to make concessions so as to mitigate the perceived risk of actual breakout. It cannot be simultaneously true that Iran is creeping towards an inherently dangerous nuclear-weapons capability *and* that the West can simply outlast Iran over an indefinite period of time: in other words, the West's own claim that time is running out also means that Iran perceives the West's bargaining position to be weaker than is assumed.

These clashing perceptions of 'stamina' – each side's perception that it can outlast the other, and therefore place the onus on the other to make concessions – result, at least *in part*, from negotiating tactics rather than deeply held beliefs. Brinkmanship is a typical component of negotiation, and it requires that a negotiating party emphasise its ability to walk away from a deal. Yet if each side conducts brinkmanship in too rigid a manner, fuelled by over-confidence, it can result in a failure to arrive at a mutually acceptable outcome – even where room for compromise exists.

Some of the factors that have encouraged brinkmanship may subside, thereby permitting a deal to be made. The US elections of November 2012, in which President Obama's political opponents adopted hard-line positions on Iran and coupled these to the electorally sensitive issue of Israeli security, greatly reduced the administration's freedom of manoeuvre. Prior to the election, American negotiators would have suffered disproportionate political costs from making, and perhaps even *floating* the idea of, concessions to Iran until after what they hoped would be re-election. With the election concluded, the US is now likely to further distance itself from Israel's vehement demands that concrete red lines for Iran's nuclear progress be articulated, for fear that such rigid criteria for military action would create unhelpful pressures for military action, and might also deprive US policy-makers of the flexibility needed in dealing with ambiguous scenarios where Iranian intent is unclear.

The nature of such electoral constraints was evident from an inadvertently revealed exchange between President Obama and Russian President Dmitri Medvedev, in which Obama confided to his counterpart that 'on all these issues, but particularly missile defense, this [US-Russia disagreement regarding missile defence] can be solved, but it's important for him [Putin] to give me space … This is my last election. After my election I have more flexibility'.[4] With the elections now concluded, and President Obama no longer concerned about re-election, there might be

---

[4] J David Goodman, 'Microphone Catches a Candid Obama', *New York Times*, 26 March 2012.

some more tangibly productive negotiation. The most important strand of this may take place directly between the US and Iran. The prospect of direct talks was leaked by US officials in the final weeks of the campaign, was alluded to by Obama in his final debate with Governor Romney, and now seems increasingly likely.

A corresponding shift is the attenuation of Iran's political fragmentation over the past two years. Iran remains divided in absolute terms, with various political factions jostling for influence. However, Mahmoud Ahmadinejad was gravely weakened in 2011 after a series of bruising clashes with the supreme leader,[5] and he found his 'principlist' faction further marginalised after the March 2012 parliamentary elections, which were dominated by factions close to Khamenei.[6] Some also argue that the ostensible rehabilitation of the pragmatic former president, Ali Akbar Hashemi Rafsanjani, in mid-2012 is suggestive of a modest consolidation in Iranian politics,[7] given that he had been pushed aside by hard-liners over the preceding years, and especially after the disputed presidential election of 2009. Khamenei's stronger political position within Iran may allow him to strike a deal with the West, less fearful of the potential domestic consequences: that the presidency would exploit the diplomatic success or that dissenting factions would take advantage of the appearance of weakness. However, others have suggested that Khamenei may also wish to avoid allowing the fruits of any diplomatic success to be accredited to Ahmadinejad, and may therefore wish to wait until June 2013, when the president's term comes to an end. This means that, even if the conditions for a deal become more propitious, this will likely take seven months or so from the time of this study's publication. Other more optimistic accounts have argued that there is in fact a window of opportunity in the final months of 2012, during which the Iranian leadership might be able to conduct effective negotiations.[8]

However, it is entirely possible that no settlement will be reached over the next twelve months at all, in which case a key question that must be asked is how stable is the status quo. Can things go on as they are, or are there forces at work that will break the deadlock, whether through resolution or conflict?

Answering this question requires an assessment of the nature and effectiveness of international pressure on Iran. Chapter II concluded that

---

[5] Muhammad Sahimi, 'Ahmadinejad-Khamenei Rift Deepens into Abyss', *PBS Frontline: Tehran Bureau*, 7 May 2011.

[6] Parisa Hafezi and Marcus George, 'Khamenei Allies Trounce Ahmadinejad in Iran Election', *Reuters*, 4 March 2012.

[7] Yasaman Baji, 'Rafsanjani's Reappointment Provokes Speculation in Iran', *Inter Press Service*, 19 March 2012.

[8] Julian Borger, 'Global Powers Launch New Push to End Iran Nuclear Crisis', *Guardian*, 11 October 2012.

there is a non-linear relationship between pressure on Iran and Iranian concessions, and that it should not be assumed that there are constantly increasing returns to Western pressure. This implies that sanctions may have bought Iran to the table in 2012, but that they cannot do all of the heavy lifting of the work yet to be done.

Compellence and Denial

Pressure has taken two forms, roughly corresponding to the distinction between 'denial' and 'compellence'. The former refers to strategies that *directly* deny an adversary's ability to pursue an undesirable policy. The latter refers to strategies that, by inflicting punishment, persuade the adversary to voluntarily alter an undesirable policy – whether that punishment is targeted specifically at the relevant policy or at some other point of pressure. Therefore, if State A occupies the territory of State B, denial would entail military action to overturn the occupation by force; compellence might involve an entirely separate blockade somewhere else, designed to increase the cost of the occupation. These two strategies have been pursued with respect to both Iran's nuclear and missile programmes.

Compellence

Compellence has mainly included sanctions, although it also incorporates measures such as asset freezes and travel bans against senior Iranian officials.

Part of the problem with assessing sanctions is that their goal is undefined. In the case of Iran, questions remain whether success can be measured as the stopping of all Iranian enrichment; the ceasing of higher-grade uranium enrichment; the dismantling of Fordow; the eliciting of Iranian co-operation with the IAEA; or some combination thereof. Western states have not specified an answer to this, and part of the reason may be that they themselves have not yet decided their 'bottom line' or, even if they have done so individually, do not agree about it.

Notwithstanding this ambiguity about what sanctions are actually for, there will arise a number of problems if sanctions are accepted as a long-term solution to the problem.

First, sanctions can induce popular dissent. A senior US intelligence official has acknowledged that the most recent round of sanctions had as one of their purposes the generation of 'enough hate and discontent at the street level so that the Iranian leaders realize that they need to change their way'.[9] However, this approach also risks inadvertently tying the hands of Western governments: domestic sensitivities in the US and other Western

---

[9] Karen DeYoung and Scott Wilson, 'Public Ire One Goal of Iran Sanctions, U.S. Official Says', *Washington Post*, 11 January 2012.

countries to the mounting regime-led repression, which would be the likely response to increased popular unrest within Iran, would constrain the policy options available to negotiators because of the perceptions entailed in dealing with an overtly repressive regime.[10] It is hard to imagine that the US Congress would support American negotiators sitting across the table from representatives of a state engaged in an active crackdown.

In other words, sanctions are designed to weaken Iran and force it to negotiate, but that weakness can bring about circumstances that hinder effective negotiation. The 2009 anti-government protests that followed Iran's presidential elections are a useful example, as they constrained President Obama's policy agenda of engaging more intensively with Iran. This is further complicated by the two-year electoral cycle in the United States, whereby presidents enjoy only a short window of opportunity in which political pressures are relaxed, before campaigning recommences.

Second, the prominence of the precedent set in Libya in 2011 means that, under conditions of major public revolt, the Iranian leadership would have every reason to focus more determinedly on the production of a nuclear weapon as a deterrent to foreign intervention and, therefore, as a guarantor of regime survival. Just because concerns over regime survival led to Iranian conciliation in 2003 does not mean it would be the case again; as explained earlier, the threat in 2003 was unique in its immediacy and credibility. By contrast, the regime's repressive capacity, demonstrated effectively in 2009, would give it every reason to think that it could suppress protest for long enough to attempt the creation of at least a rudimentary deterrent capability.

More broadly, the twin policies of holding the regime at risk and pursuing regime change are easily blurred – both in the sense that the former policy may *appear to Iran* indistinguishable from regime change, and in the sense that it may in fact *become* functionally equivalent to a policy of regime change in ways that are hard to judge and finesse.

This does not mean that the military threat against Iran is irrelevant: Iran might well be deterred from overtly seeking nuclear weapons for fear that intense, sustained and prolonged air strikes (like those faced by Iraq in the 1990s) would be truly regime-threatening on a timeline that precluded the production of a nuclear deterrent before political disintegration. However, sanctions are much slower acting than this, and the Iranian regime's capacity to absorb pressure over a longer period is very considerable. After all, 'during the height of its war with Iraq, Iran's annual oil revenues fell under $6 billion – less than ten per cent of its 2010 take'.[11] This resilience may enable a longer period of nuclear gestation.

---

[10] I am grateful to Malcolm Chalmers for this point.
[11] Suzanne Maloney, 'Obama's Counterproductive New Iran Sanctions', *Foreign Affairs*, 5 January 2012.

Furthermore, if the regime is also threatened from within anyway, then it is more likely to take the risk of inviting the military action that would likely follow nuclear breakout. It is possible, therefore, that Iran assesses that it could survive air strikes, rally regime support, and then reconstitute a nuclear programme outside the auspices of the IAEA.

The third problem with sanctions is that high levels of pressure can alter the domestic balance of power, by validating the hard-liners' contention that Iran's adversaries are interested less in a settlement of the nuclear issue and more in regime change. In 2003, as Iran faced European pressure and possible referral to the UN Security Council, a multifaceted debate took place within and between Iran's domestic political institutions. As nuclear negotiator Hassan Rowhani recalls, 'some believed that cooperation with Europe would not have any effect on the situation' but 'there also were those who believed that cooperation with Europe could bear fruit'.[12] As sanctions tighten, and the sense of being under siege heightens, it will be harder for those who hold the latter, more conciliatory positions to persuade their less-flexible colleagues to make concessions.

Fourth, sanctions are beset by a number of other problems. They risk empowering those regime-associated actors able to profit from smuggling networks – in the case of Iran, this includes the IRGC and related factions – and weakening potential private-sector counterweights to state power.[13] Sanctions also impact the general populace, potentially generating enormous humanitarian costs that, in turn, make the sanctions and the governments imposing those sanctions politically unpopular, both within the targeted state and outside. The 1990s sanctions on Iraq, for example, gravely exacerbated child mortality, eroded civilian infrastructure and, despite their initial popularity in parts of the Arab world, became a major grievance against Western foreign policy.[14]

These problems do not mean that sanctions are entirely ineffective; indeed, sanctions are undoubtedly having an impact on Iran's economy. Food prices, inflation and unemployment have all sharply increased.[15] Iranian oil exports have been cut by at least a quarter (with revenues down by 35 per cent) since the beginning of 2012, which will result in

---

[12] Rowhani, 'Beyond the Challenges Facing Iran and the IAEA Concerning the Nuclear Dossier', speech to the Supreme Cultural Revolution Council, trans. FBIS, *Rahbord*, 30 September 2005, p. 6, <http://lewis.armscontrolwonk.com/files/2012/08/Rahbord.pdf>, accessed 19 October 2012.

[13] Daniel Byman and Matthew Waxman, *The Dynamics of Coercion: American Foreign Policy and the Limits of Military Might* (Cambridge: Cambridge University Press, 2002), pp. 105–17.

[14] Joy Gordon, 'Lessons We Should Have Learned from the Iraqi Sanctions', *Foreign Policy*, 8 July 2010.

[15] Najmeh Bozorgmehr, 'Sanctions Threaten Weak Iranian Economy', *Financial Times*, 27 June 2012.

approximately $10 billion of foregone revenues. Surplus oil (roughly a million barrels per day) is being forced into storage on tankers, but two-thirds of the Iranian tanker fleet are now reportedly in use for this purpose.[16] President Ahmadinejad, having earlier played down the significance of sanctions, now acknowledges that 'the sanctions imposed on our country are the most severe and strictest sanctions ever imposed on a country'.[17]

There is also some evidence that the sanctions imposed on Iran have altered popular perceptions. A poll of Iranians on a state news website found that 63 per cent of respondents wanted 'the suspension of uranium enrichment in exchange for gradual lifting of sanctions'.[18] Although the poll is itself obviously unreliable given its source, was later retracted, and appears to contradict earlier surveys of public opinion that have found deep support for a peaceful nuclear programme, its very publication may be telling.

However, Iranian leaders have repeatedly and publicly articulated that the right to enrich (not just import) fuel is a red line in negotiations, and that sanctions will not produce Iranian submission on what is presented, in part, as an inalienable right and therefore a basic point of principle.[19] Although it is clearly impossible to say with certainty, sanctions – no matter how punitive – are unlikely to force Iranian submission on this point. Moreover, there is no significant political grouping within Iran, not even reformists, who would favour abandoning Iran's enrichment programme on pain of sanctions. Many of the proponents of sanctions in the West have engaged in wishful thinking in this regard.

Denial
Denial policy, targeted squarely at the nuclear and missile programmes rather than the broader economy, has included a formal export-control regime (such as the Nuclear Suppliers Group), an aggressive but informal technology-denial regime, sabotage of nuclear- and missile-related infrastructure and supply chains, and other forms of covert action, such as the assassination of Iranian nuclear scientists and cyber-warfare targeting Iranian centrifuges. The purpose of the denial strategy has been not only to increase the cost of Iran's nuclear programme beyond a

---

[16] Thomas Erdbrink and Clifford Krauss, 'Oil Backed Up, Iranians Put it on Idled Ships', *New York Times*, 4 July 2012.
[17] Thomas Erdbrink and Rick Gladstone, 'Iran's President Says New Sanctions Are Toughest Yet', *New York Times*, 3 July 2012.
[18] Hossein Bastani, 'Iran Poll Draws Startling Response to Nuclear Question', *BBC News*, 5 July 2012.
[19] David Ignatius, 'A Breakdown in Iran Nuclear Talks Appears Likely', *Washington Post*, 3 July 2012.

level deemed beneficial to the regime, but also to *retard* nuclear- and missile-related programmes in order to buy time for the compellence strategies to take effect. (A further advantage of denial efforts is that, in monitoring Iranian efforts to procure proliferation-relevant material, they provide greater information on the nature of the Iranian programme itself.)

Cyber-warfare against Iran's nuclear programme, which began during the George W Bush administration, peaked with the pioneering Stuxnet virus, reportedly developed by the US and Israel. This forced the decommissioning and replacement of at least a fifth of Iran's then-5,000 operating centrifuges and, according to internal administration estimates, delayed the Iranian nuclear programme by eighteen months to two years.[20] This supplemented earlier efforts, led by the CIA, to inject faulty parts and designs into Iran's nuclear programme.[21] The assassination of five Iranian nuclear scientists over the past five years, allegedly by Israeli agents, is likewise intended both to deter Iranian scientists from working on the nuclear programme and to eliminate those with specialist knowledge.[22] Additionally, there have occurred a series of explosions at Iranian facilities, including two in November 2011 at a missile base to the west of Tehran and the Isfahan uranium-conversion facility.[23]

Although the United States insists that it does not conduct 'kinetic activity inside Iran', it has worked closely with Israel to the point where the US National Security Advisor Thomas Donilon has observed that 'I don't think you've ever seen the intelligence and military coordination happen at a more intense level in any previous administration'. Nevertheless, US officials commonly hold Israel responsible for the most prominent acts of assassination and sabotage.[24]

The various facets of this denial regime have undoubtedly contributed to a slower pace of uranium enrichment and missile development than would otherwise have been the case. In July 2012, the head of Britain's Secret Intelligence Service (SIS), Sir John Sawers, claimed that his organisation, and its allied counterparts, had 'run a series of operations to ensure that the sanctions [against Iran] introduced internationally are implemented', and that, consequently, 'Iranian nuclear development has been significantly

---

[20] David E Sanger, 'Obama Ordered Sped Up Wave of Cyberattacks Against Iran', *New York Times*, 1 June 2012.

[21] Scott Shane, 'Adversaries of Iran Said to Be Stepping Up Covert Actions', *New York Times*, 11 January 2012.

[22] Artin Afkhami, 'Tehran Abuzz as Book Says Israel Killed 5 Scientists', *New York Times*, 11 July 2012.

[23] Saeed Kamali Dehghan, 'Iran: Explosion in Isfahan Reported', *Guardian*, 28 November 2011.

[24] David E Sanger, *Confront and Conceal: Obama's Secret Wars and the Surprising Use of American Power* (New York: Crown, 2012), pp. 144–45.

delayed by the international community: in 2003, Iran was believed to be five years away from having the bomb; but nearly a decade later, they're still thought to have two years to go'.[25]

For instance, Iran has been compelled to use lower-quality metal for its centrifuges, substituting carbon fibre for maraging steel in key parts.[26] Another report, by the London-based International Institute for Strategic Studies, judges that 'sanctions continue to disrupt Tehran's access to the key propellant ingredients and components needed to produce large solid-propellant rocket motors', to the point that Iran's long-range missile programme has been severely hampered.[27]

At the same time, Iran has adapted to these forms of pressure, even though this has cost more in terms of both time and resources. Iran has sought alternative supply chains for centrifuge parts, has afforded greater protection to nuclear scientists, and has likely responded by better defending its nuclear infrastructure against further physical and cyber attack. As David Sanger notes, 'a review of Iran's production records, released by the IAEA, suggests that by speeding up the centrifuges that were still working, Iran's output of enriched uranium did not decline' as a result of the attack using Stuxnet.[28] Assassinated scientists are not irreplaceable, as shown by the Israeli assassinations of Iraqi scientists in the 1970s and 1980s that did not prevent Iraq from nuclear advances (which is why Israel eventually decided to launch air strikes anyway).

Although offensive covert action will continue to be a key part of Western policy, it will have variable and likely diminishing returns, as Iran flexibly responds and defends itself. Denial efforts have delayed, but cannot halt, the enrichment programme. Western policy-makers regard these delays as being worthwhile because, in lengthening the time it would take Iran to acquire nuclear weapons, they buy time both for diplomacy to have an effect and for sanctions to bite. However, this means that denial plays, at best, a secondary role to compellence, merely buying time for sanctions to impose an increasing cost.

It should also be noted that the denial regime itself is not without costs. First, it consumes large amounts of intelligence resources that could be allocated elsewhere. According to the 2011–12 report of the UK

---

[25] Christopher Hope, 'MI6 Chief Sir John Sawers: "We Foiled Iranian Nuclear Weapons Bid"', *Daily Telegraph*, 12 July 2012; for a broader perspective on the scope and effectiveness of the denial effort, see David Vielhaber and Philipp C Bleek, 'Shadow Wars: Covert Operations Against Iran's Nuclear Program', *Nonproliferation Review* (Vol. 19, No. 3, November 2012).

[26] David Albright and Christina Walrond, 'Iran's Advanced Centrifuges', ISIS Report, 18 October 2011.

[27] Alexander Nicoll (ed.), 'Iran: Sanctions Halt Long-Range Ballistic-Missile Development', *IISS Strategic Comments* (Vol. 18, July 2012).

[28] Sanger, *Confront and Conceal*, p. 207.

parliament's Intelligence and Security Committee, the SIS declared that its coverage of individual Arab states had been in decline 'for some time', and that its priorities in relation to the Middle East were counter-terrorism and Iran. This naturally left intelligence gaps during the progression of the Arab Spring.[29] Furthermore, although the US faces a less severe budget constraint than the UK, it, too, has deployed a considerable proportion of its intelligence and national security resources to Iran-related challenges.

Second, Iran has retaliated to the use of covert action. For example, in February 2012, Iran was alleged to be responsible for a series of attempted attacks on Israeli diplomats in New Delhi, Bangkok and Tbilisi, and it was held responsible, by Israel and the US, for a further attack against Israeli tourists in Bulgaria.[30] However, if these incidents were indeed acts of Iranian retaliation, they are suggestive of a far more limited retaliatory capability than has sometimes been attributed to Tehran. Of the first wave, only the Delhi attack was even partially successful, and that, too, failed in directly affecting any Israeli diplomats.

Third, and finally, covert action contributes to a sense of being under siege that can be exploited by Iranian leaders so as to increase popular support for the nuclear programme and to reinforce the narrative that Iran is under foreign attack. In other words, denial can result in many of the same adverse consequences, detailed earlier, that may result from a long-term entrenchment of sanctions.

Regime Destabilisation
Straddling both denial and compellence has been a more extreme form of pressure: avowed efforts at regime destabilisation, separate from the nuclear programme. In a 2007 meeting with US Under Secretary of State for Political Affairs Nicholas Burns, then-Mossad chief Meir Dagan specified that one of Israel's 'pillars' for dealing with Iran also included an effort to overthrow the government: 'Dagan said that more should be done to foment regime change in Iran, possibly with the support of student democracy movements, and ethnic groups (e.g., Azeris, Kurds, Baluchs [*sic*]) opposed to the ruling regime...Dagan urged more attention on regime change, asserting that more could be done to develop the identities of ethnic minorities in Iran' so that Iran 'could become a normal state'.[31] Such policies, which obviously impose a cost on Iran but can only have an

---

[29] Intelligence and Security Committee, *Annual Report 2011–2012*, Cm 8403 (London: The Stationery Office, 2012).
[30] Nicholas Kulish and Eric Schmitt, 'Hezbollah Is Blamed in Attack on Israeli Tourists in Bulgaria', *New York Times*, 19 July 2012.
[31] US embassy, Tel Aviv, 'U/S Burns' August 17 Meeting With Israeli Mossad Chief Meir Dagan', 31 August 2007, <http://cables.mrkva.eu/cable.php?id=120696>, accessed 24 October 2012.

effect over a long period of time, also risk making the regime less secure, and therefore increasing the value of a nuclear deterrent.

The Military Option

In its most extreme form, the denial regime could include a direct military attack on Iranian nuclear facilities. Ronen Bergman, an Israeli investigative journalist, concluded a widely read January 2012 assessment by noting that, 'after speaking with many senior Israeli leaders and chiefs of the military and the intelligence, I have come to believe that Israel will indeed strike Iran in 2012'.[32] In March 2012, President Obama responded to a wave of anticipation of an Israeli strike by declaring that 'both the Iranian and the Israeli governments recognize that when the United States says it is unacceptable for Iran to have a nuclear weapon, we mean what we say', and that 'a military component' would remain an option.[33]

The likelihood and effectiveness of a military strike is extremely important, because it forms the backdrop to ongoing negotiations. If a strike is probable and likely to be effective, then – notwithstanding the regime-consolidating effects of such a strike – Iran has greater incentives to concede to Western demands. By contrast, if a strike is either improbable or likely to be ineffective, then Iran is better able to reject Western demands and ride out the status quo to its own advantage.

There are a number of reasons to question both the probability and the effectiveness of an Israeli military strike. First, Israel has every incentive to exaggerate its willingness to strike, both in order to dissuade Iran from nuclear advances and to spur on US and European pressure against Iran. In the past, Israeli threats have indeed proven to be bluffs. Many of the purported triggering conditions for an Israeli strike – for instance, a belief in the imminence of Iran's immunity from military action – have been reached before, multiple times, without leading to Israeli military action.[34]

Second, and a related point, Israel's leadership is itself divided on the merits of a strike. Former Mossad chief Meir Dagan, an influential voice on national security affairs, famously criticised a military strike as 'the stupidest idea' he had ever heard and, despite a partial retraction of those comments, continued to oppose a strike. Former IDF chiefs of staff, former chiefs of the internal Shin Bet intelligence agency, and other national security elites have also been vocally opposed to a unilateral strike.

Third, Prime Minister Benjamin Netanyahu has exhibited consistent risk-aversion. As Daniel Levy notes, referring to operations carried out

---

[32] Ronen Bergman, 'Will Israel Attack Iran?', *New York Times*, 25 January 2012.

[33] *BBC News*, 'Obama Warns Against Pre-Emptive Iran Strike', 2 March 2012.

[34] Jeffrey Goldberg, 'Will Israel Attack Iran This Year?', *Atlantic Monthly*, 25 January 2012. Goldberg himself had earlier predicted that Israel would strike in spring 2011.

under previous Israeli administrations, there have been 'no Operation Cast Leads, Lebanon wars, or Syria ... attack missions under [Netanyahu's] watch. In fact, he has no record of military adventurism'. Nor have Netanyahu's right-wing political allies been enthusiastic at the prospect of military action, in part because 'the more settler-centric right is also cognizant of the distraction value served by the Iranian nuclear issue in deflecting attention from its land grabs and entrenchment in the West Bank and East Jerusalem'.[35] The July 2012 withdrawal of the Kadima party from Israel's unity government has further increased Netanyahu's political vulnerability, as has the opposition of Israeli President Shimon Peres to acting without US approval.[36]

Fourth, regardless of the probability of a military strike, it remains a fundamentally counterproductive choice of policy. Unless Israel is able to mount simultaneous raids by special forces or crippling acts of sabotage targeting Iranian facilities – something that should not be ruled out – it would have to rely on airpower or missile strikes, or perhaps both, even if augmented by preparatory cyber-attacks.

However, it would face problems of overflying around 1,000 miles of partially unfriendly airspace, insufficient aerial refuelling aircraft, and the penetration or circumvention of Iranian air defences, as well as the possibility that Iranian resistance would either deplete a strike force en route, thereby limiting the damage that could be done, or deplete the returning aircraft. Former CIA director Michael V Hayden has said that effective air strikes remain 'beyond the capacity' of Israel, in part because Israel's most effective munitions, the 5,000-pound GBU-28 'bunker buster' bombs, would not be guaranteed to penetrate to sufficient depth the underground facility at Fordow.[37] According to estimates derived from US war games, an initial Israeli attack would set back the Iranian nuclear programme by roughly a year.[38] A large working group of former senior national security officials estimated that Israel could delay the programme by up to two years, and would be 'unlikely to succeed in destroying or even seriously damaging' Fordow without improbable ground attacks.[39]

A US strike would be more effective, both because of its ability to mount repeated attacks and to assess carefully the damage inflicted between attacks, as well as the penetrativity of its munitions. However,

---

[35] Daniel Levy, 'Netanyahu Won't Attack Iran', *Foreign Policy*, 2 March 2012.

[36] Shai Feldman, 'The Israeli Debate on Attacking Iran is Over', *Foreign Policy*, 20 August 2012.

[37] Elisabeth Bumiller, 'Iran Raid Seen as a Huge Task for Israeli Jets', *New York Times*, 19 February 2012.

[38] Mark Mazzetti and Thom Shanker, 'U.S. War Game Sees Perils of Israeli Strike against Iran', *New York Times*, 19 March 2012.

[39] Wilson Center, 'Weighing the Benefits and Costs of Military Action against Iran', 13 September 2012, p. 25.

as former Secretary of Defense Robert Gates has acknowledged, 'the reality is that there is no military option that does anything more than buy time – the estimates are three years or so'.[40] The CIA's assessment of physical attack options was that 'none of them looked workable', prompting the US to inform Israel that 'an attack would just drive the program more underground . . . the inspectors would be thrown out. The Iranians would rebuild, more determined than ever. And eventually, they would achieve their objective'.[41]

This is the problem that lies at the core of the military option: it does not represent a solution, but merely a delaying tactic. It carries with it the near certainty of the expulsion of IAEA inspectors, presently the best means of detecting any diversion of enriched uranium for weapons purposes, the possibility of (perfectly legal) Iranian withdrawal from the NPT, and the likelihood that Iran would reconstitute its nuclear programme, albeit with some difficulty, in covert form. The two counterarguments to this are first, that Iran could simply be struck again in a series of actions that Israelis have called, in a grimly casual phrase, 'mowing the lawn';[42] and, second, that even a short delay would allow sanctions to bite, which would either collapse a politically fragile regime (and, it is implied, produce a more conciliatory government) or force the regime to abandon enrichment in order to mitigate the pressure on itself.[43] Yet neither of these arguments is persuasive.

One reason for this is that Iran now possesses the ability to indigenously make centrifuges: 'it does not need to shop abroad, and its knowledge is well formalized in internal documents and spread among hundreds of engineers'. This means that, in the aftermath of any strike, 'if Iran's infrastructure were dismantled, intelligence sources lost, people repurposed, telephones disconnected, and computers networks shut down, then there would be significantly less insight into Iran's activities, and accordingly less confidence going forward that Iran had not reconstituted a new program'.[44]

Currently, Iran wholly accepts the inspections regime, to which it is treaty-bound, and frequently refers to it as an indicator of its peaceful intentions. The inspections regime is not perfect, but it does guarantee that fissile material cannot realistically be diverted without detection. In February 2012, the IAEA announced that Iran had not accounted for a small

[40] David E Sanger and William J Broad, 'U.S. and Allies Warn Iran over Nuclear "Deception"', *New York Times*, 25 September 2009.
[41] Sanger, *Confront and Conceal*, pp. 229–30.
[42] Steven Simon, 'An Israeli Strike on Iran', Contingency Planning Memorandum No. 5, Council on Foreign Relations, November 2009, p. 3.
[43] Matthew Kroenig, 'Time to Attack Iran: Why a Strike is the Least Bad Option', *Foreign Affairs* (Vol. 91, No. 1, January/February 2012).
[44] Bill Keller, 'How About Not Bombing Iran?', *New York Times*, 22 January 2012.

discrepancy (19.8 kg) between its declared and measured stocks of natural uranium metal and process waste. In May 2012, the agency found traces of highly enriched uranium on Iranian equipment. This was almost certainly a benign technical problem rather than evidence of breakout. However, both of these episodes suggest that the IAEA is capable of detecting Iranian transgressions of the sort that would be necessary for producing the fissile material required to build nuclear weapons.

An opaquely reconstituted programme would create uncertainty over issues that are clear and transparent today – for instance, the quantity, location and enrichment-level of Iran's uranium stockpile. Even if repeated strikes against Iran's nuclear infrastructure ('mowing the lawn') were therefore politically advisable – and they are categorically not, given the great human cost and regional instability that such attacks would incur – they may not even be technically possible, because human intelligence sources, however impressive, could only report a limited amount about new, covert sites. In other words, there is reason to expect sharply diminishing returns between the first and second, and further, rounds of air strikes. Moreover, the worsening of Iranian threat perceptions and fear of further strikes could shift Iran's calculus decisively in favour of a nuclear weapon – a weapon that, according to both the United States and Israel, it has *not* yet decided to actually build.

Defenders of military action retort with the argument that military action would produce a sufficient delay for sanctions to effect regime change before Iran was able to reconstitute its nuclear activities to their present level. However, the poor historic record of sanctions in inducing regime change or drastic policy shifts suggests that there should be no confidence in the view that Iran would be toppled or decisively squeezed before it was successful in producing weapons.

Although a post-strike Iran would certainly be subject to the same technology-denial regime to which it is subject now, and might therefore struggle to re-source parts and materials that it had first obtained over the 1990s and 2000s, this would probably not be sufficient to prevent a reconstitution of its nuclear programme.

The notion that Iran would simply 'quit the nuclear game altogether', as suggested by Matthew Kroenig, is implausible. Kroenig invokes the precedents of Iraq after the First Gulf War and Syria after Israel's 2007 strike on its half-constructed reactor.[45] However, both of these are misleading analogies. Only a major land war, of the sort that simply will not occur against Iran, curbed Iraqi ambitions, and Syria's nuclear programme was at a far more incipient stage – concentrated in a single, vulnerable site – than Iran's sprawling, hardened nuclear infrastructure.

---

[45] Kroenig, 'Time to Attack Iran'.

A better, if still imperfect, precedent is Israel's 1981 raid on Iraq's Osirak reactor. According to the most recent scholarship, which draws on the testimony of scientists involved with the Iraqi nuclear programme, Israel's military action 'triggered a nuclear weapons program where one did not previously exist, while forcing Iraq to pursue a more difficult and time-consuming technological route', such that 'within a decade Iraq stood on the threshold of a nuclear weapons capability'. After the strike, between 1983 and 1991, the nuclear programme's staff increased by 60 per cent every year, and Saddam Hussein increased the resources allocated by around twenty-five times.[46]

Moreover, after the strike, Iraq's 'key priority was to develop a program with a small signature (i.e., one that would be difficult to detect by other states)'.[47] In short, Iraq did not respond to a strike by winding down its programme and quitting the nuclear game, but by turning a haphazard and directionless programme into a determined, better-resourced and better-hidden quest for nuclear weapons. That pursuit was frustrated by a course of events – the Iraqi invasion of Kuwait and the overwhelming international response – that was *sui generis* and that would not be replicable in the case of Iran. Proponents of an attack on Iran have supplied no evidence to suggest that Iran would react to a strike any differently to Iraq.

Compromise

It is increasingly clear that a zero-enrichment solution, one in which Iran capitulates on its core interest, is out of reach, and that the P5 + 1's collective insistence on this condition will result either in a futile protraction of what have aptly been called 'zombie talks';[48] or a breakdown of those talks and a continuation of Iranian enrichment and economic disintegration; or, worst of all, an Israeli military strike that engenders a covert Iranian drive for weaponisation.[49]

It is possible that the status quo can remain for years; but this is an undesirable outcome. Although Iran would be subject to the same tripwires against nuclear breakout it faces now, the risks posed by its programme, as perceived by the West, would also grow: it would have more enriched uranium, more enrichment capacity, more advanced missile capability, and – depending on what one believes about its post-2003

---

[46] Malfrid Braut-Hegghammer, 'Revisiting Osirak: Preventive Attacks and Nuclear Proliferation Risks', *International Security* (Vol. 36, No. 1, Summer 2011), p. 102.
[47] *Ibid.*, pp. 117–18.
[48] Julian Borger, 'Iran Nuclear Negotiations: The Dawn of The Zombie Talks', *Guardian*, 20 June 2012.
[49] Matthew Bunn, 'Beyond Zero Enrichment: Suggestions for an Iranian Nuclear Deal', Belfer Center Policy Brief, Harvard Kennedy School, November 2009.

weapons research – more familiarity with how to turn fissile material into a bomb. The risk of destabilising Israeli military action would remain or even increase, obviating one of the purposes of imposing sanctions. A compromise agreement, by which Iran's nuclear programme came to be seen as less threatening, is therefore important.

However, if the P5 + 1 is to reverse a position it has held for years and has articulated in various UN Security Council resolutions, it must be considered how it can do this in a way that addresses these states' concerns over a future Iranian breakout for weapons. The following suggestions do not represent a blueprint, but merely some principles that should guide the type of settlement that would best address such matters.

First, it should be recognised that *some* limits on Iranian enrichment are better than *no* limits, because this elongates Iran's breakout timeline. The focus should therefore be on uranium enrichment to 20 per cent, which shortens Iran's breakout timeline far more than lower-grade enrichment. This is because uranium enriched to 20 per cent, MEU, is not 20 per cent of the way to weapons-grade, as the nomenclature suggests, but is in fact *90 per cent* of the way, as was explained in Chapter II. Western policy-makers would prefer a situation in which Iran has a given stockpile of uranium enriched to 3.5 per cent (LEU) instead of a *smaller* stockpile of MEU, because it would take disproportionately longer for Iran to enrich the first stockpile to weapons-grade, a prerequisite for making weapons.

Capping Iran's enrichment to lower levels is the most feasible way of slowing down any future attempt to produce nuclear weapons. Allowing lower-grade enrichment satisfies Iran's core demand, allows Iranian leaders to sell any deal to domestic audiences as a diplomatic victory, and undercuts the Iranian complaint that its fundamental rights are being curtailed. The P5 + 1 should offer sanctions relief – though, importantly, not sanctions *removal* – in return for Iran accepting such a cap (as should have been done in June 2012, at the talks in Moscow). An Iranian agreement to stop and shut down enrichment at Fordow should also be met with the provision of fuel plates for Iran's research reactor, and preparations for such provision should be made immediately. (One of the problems with the 2009 fuel swap was the gap between Iran handing over its uranium and its receipt of fabricated fuel.)

During the Moscow talks in June 2012, the suggestion by the US and some European states that Iran would not receive sanctions relief even if it did shut down Fordow and end enrichment to 20 per cent was a serious error. Iran was left with little incentive to make a concession, especially given that Iran's stockpile of uranium enriched to 20 per cent is its most important bargaining chip. Moreover, asking Iran to shut Fordow is tantamount to asking for hostages, in the sense that it constitutes a demand that Iran concentrate its enrichment activity in Natanz, a site that is more easily bombed. The P5 + 1 should also explore alternatives to shutting Fordow, such as a voluntary but drastic reduction in the number of centrifuges – something that would have much the same effect.

Second, the P5 + 1 should not emphasise stockpiles of enriched uranium, whether LEU or MEU, at the expense of other concerns. MEU is important because it can technically be quickly enriched to weapons-grade fissile material, whether at safeguarded or secret sites. However, as Chapter II of this study emphasised, what matters is not just how quickly Iran can produce fissile material and then a weapon, but also the likelihood of detection as it does so. Negotiations should therefore prioritise verification mechanisms that provide the IAEA with better visibility into Iran's enrichment activity and any broader nuclear activity that would be relevant to producing a warhead.

The most valuable steps in this direction would be, first, Iran's re-application of modified Code 3.1 of its Subsidiary Arrangements with the IAEA which obliges Iran to report the construction of new nuclear facilities, and second, Iran's ratification and re-adoption of the Additional Protocol to its Safeguards Agreement, which gives the IAEA broader powers of verification. Iran should be offered further, but still limited, sanctions relief in exchange for each of these concessions.

These are not a panacea – after all, Iran signed an Additional Protocol in 2003 and implemented it until 2006, without the dispute being resolved – but they are crucial. That is because, in enabling more frequent and intrusive inspections, these measures make it far more likely that breakout would be detected. Moreover, the Additional Protocol also increases the probability of finding any covert nuclear facilities, because it allows the IAEA to collect environmental samples at locations other than declared sites and to build up a better picture of the Iranian nuclear programme as a whole.[50] The IAEA's difficulty in securing access to sites like Parchin, where Iran is suspected of having conducted implosion tests relevant to the development of a bomb, would be greatly eased if Iran was still adhering to the AP. Iran has offered what it calls the 'operationalisation' of the supreme leader's fatwa against nuclear weapons as a concession, but it must understand that, with the fatwa itself being easily reversible and therefore of negligible worth, the only real means of such 'operationalisation' will be such intrusive verification measures.[51]

---

[50] Geoffrey Forden and John Thomson, 'Iran as a Pioneer Case for Multilateral Nuclear Arrangements', Science, Technology, and Global Security Working Group, Massachusetts Institute of Technology, May 2009, p. 9.

[51] On the fatwa's limited value, see Michael Eisenstadt and Mehdi Khalaji, 'Nuclear Fatwa: Religion and Politics in Iranisenstadt and Mehdi Khala', Policy Focus No. 15, Washington Institute for Near East Policy, September 2011, ch. 2.

Fourth, and closely related to the issue of verification, Iran must address the IAEA's concerns over alleged military dimensions to the nuclear programme, as described earlier in this Whitehall Paper. This would allow the IAEA to offer what is known as a 'broader conclusion' that Iran's programme is wholly peaceful; but this can only be done with greater transparency, forthrightness and openness from Iran.

However, it is likely that at least some of these allegations – such as those concerning nuclear weapons research in the late 1990s and early 2000s – are correct. Iran might therefore fear that any admission of weapons-related activity would not resolve the issue, but simply vindicate Western demands that it suspend all enrichment. Therefore, regardless of the propriety or prudence of such a demand, the priority should be to validate and guarantee Iran's *present* peaceful intentions, instead of uncovering *past* activity. In some cases, of course, these are inseparable: the IAEA must be able to interview scientists involved with the alleged weapons programme prior to 2003, in order to understand whether and how their work has changed over time. However, it should be borne in mind that a number of states – including many Western allies – have had clandestine weapons programmes, which were later abandoned. As such, the focus should be on what Iran is doing now.

Therefore, the P5 + 1 should consider offering Iran an amnesty or 'grace period' regarding past weapons-related work.[52] It appears that Western diplomats are open to this offer, conditional on Iran adopting stringent verification mechanisms and co-operating in good faith with the IAEA.[53]

Any process of verification would take time, given the volume of evidence against Iran that the IAEA has accumulated, and the depth of mistrust between the two parties. Western states want Iran to stop the enrichment of uranium while this process is underway and, although this would be hard for Iran to stomach, it is not a fanciful suggestion. Such a moratorium, rather than indefinite suspension, even forms part of a relatively sympathetic Russian proposal to Iran.[54] A moratorium would allow the P5 + 1 to claim that UN Security Council resolutions have been respected, and Iran could plausibly claim it was doing no more than repeating a gesture it had made in 2003. Ultimately, Iran must understand

---

[52] The importance of an amnesty has been evident for a long time. Even in 2003, for instance, those Iranian decision-makers who favoured co-operation and transparency were understandably concerned that this would give the United States a pretext for further pressure instead of reward. See Rowhani, 'Beyond the Challenges Facing Iran and the IAEA Concerning the Nuclear Dossier'.

[53] *NTI.org*, 'Experts Call for Concessions to Allow U.N. Nuclear Probe in Iran', 16 July 2012.

[54] Seyed Hossein Mousavian, *The Iranian Nuclear Crisis: A Memoir* (Washington, DC: Carnegie Endowment for International Peace, 2012), p. 408.

that, even if it earned sanctions relief in return for interim steps, sanctions will not be completely lifted until it is given a clean bill of health by the IAEA.

Fifth, negotiations should be undertaken with greater effort at maintaining secrecy. Major diplomatic agreements require each side to be able to float ideas, suggest concessions and engage in a vigorous back-and-forth without fear of these details leaking to the press, with the result being the appearance of weakness in the eyes of domestic audiences. The most recent rounds of negotiations have been characterised by day-by-day leaks to the international press, making it harder for the West to propose sanctions relief (particularly in an election year in the US) and harder for Iran to propose bold curbs on its enrichment. Given the difficulty of preserving secrecy with such a large number of participants, it would be in both sides' interests to conduct backchannel talks between the United States and the office of the supreme leader. Furthermore, given the risk of leaks, this can only realistically begin now that the US presidential elections have concluded.

These five principles, taken together, suggest that it is possible to imagine a carefully sequenced and graduated (rather than all-in-one) deal between Iran and the P5 + 1 unfolding most probably after June 2013, involving incremental sanctions relief and the de facto recognition from the West of Iran's right to enrich uranium to lower levels, and stringent verification measures, curbs on higher-grade enrichment and co-operation with the IAEA from Iran. At each step, backsliding would be possible, as would the re-imposition or intensification of sanctions.

The entire process could be disrupted by anti-regime protests in Iran, air strikes against Iranian nuclear sites or an abortive Iranian attempt at breakout. However, talks are not fated to fail. A settlement would require both sides to take bold and politically risky steps. Of course, the effect of sanctions on Iran, and political developments within each country, may very well preclude this. However, as argued above, that would result in a long-term stand-off, the entrenchment of crippling sanctions, and the dangerous accumulation of tensions around Iran's expanding nuclear programme.

It should be noted that Israel and the more sceptical members of the P5 + 1 are worried that Iran will use a short-term deal to stall for time and release some of the pressure on itself.[55] This is indeed a risk but, even if Iran does have malign intentions, capping its enrichment *automatically* puts Iran further away from nuclear weapons. Moreover, sanctions relief can be made commensurate to the scale of the Iranian concession. The EU does not have to reverse its oil embargo *in toto*, although this, too, should eventually

---

[55] Laura Rozen, 'US Mulls Seeking Broader Deal In Nuclear Talks With Iran', *Al-Monitor*, 7 June 2012.

be an option on the table, but it could relax parts of the sanctions, such as the restrictions on insurance provision for Iranian oil shipments. This more limited form of sanctions relief would both be easily reversible, if necessary, and would still leave Iran under considerable pressure from the weight of other sanctions. Indeed, the failure to sub-divide concessions on each side has been a lost opportunity in negotiations; and, although some would criticise the idea of any Iranian enrichment as unacceptably dangerous, the fact remains that the status quo entails a growing Iranian nuclear programme, and any proposed deal must be measured against that alternative.

Finally, there is one further aspect to any settlement: whether and how it deals with the underlying security competition between Iran and its adversaries. This has long been a part of negotiations. Aside from Iran's 2003 Swiss-conveyed suggestion of a grand bargain, discussed in Chapter II, there have been many other, more modest efforts at limited rapprochement.[56]

In 2003, the EU3 pledged to 'co-operate with Iran to promote security and stability in the region including the establishment of a zone free from weapons of mass destruction in the Middle East'. In the 2004 Paris agreement, they promised 'firm commitments on security issues', to be fleshed out by 'working groups on political and security issues'. Then, in 2005, the Europeans responded to various proposals that Iran had submitted to those working groups, by offering its own detailed suggestions: 'The [EU3] recognise that they share a number of specific security concerns and interests with Iran and the important role Iran can potentially play in ensuring regional security and stability', including in the areas of Iraq, Afghanistan, counter-terrorism and counternarcotics. They proposed that these be developed through 'the creation of a high-level committee on political and security issues, which would be made up of representatives from respective Foreign Affairs and Defence authorities'.

Iran has been, and remains, enthusiastic about the institutionalisation of security co-operation. While its critics suggest that this is to deflect attention from the nuclear file, its defenders retort that it stems from Iranian hesitance to offer unilateral assistance that may be pocketed without reward, as with Iran's efforts in Afghanistan just after 2001.[57] Either way, Western diplomats remain unconvinced that security co-operation can surpass merely tactical co-operation because, on a number of core issues, they see Iran as having irredeemably malign intentions. The latest manifestation of this mistrust has been Iran's exclusion from international

---

[56] *Armscontrol.org*, 'History of Official Proposals on the Iranian Nuclear Issue', last updated August 2012.
[57] Trita Parsi, *A Single Roll of the Dice: Obama's Diplomacy with Iran* (New Haven, CT: Yale University Press, 2012), Kindle edition, locations 782–812 (ch. 3).

talks about Syria, despite the wishes of the then-mediator, former UN Secretary General Kofi Annan, that Iranian representatives be present.[58]

A further concern is that institutionalising security co-operation with Iran would legitimise its role in the Gulf, including those activities – such as assistance to Hizbullah and Hamas – that are seen as inimical both to Western interests, but also to those of Western allies in the region. In particular, Arab states have long feared and opposed any arrangement that would increase Iranian prestige, influence and visibility in the region, because they see this as tantamount to the destabilisation of their own regimes and the encouragement of Iran's hegemonic ambitions.

At the Baghdad talks in May 2012, for instance, Iran sought to include Syria and Bahrain in the discussions. However, any suggestion of an Iranian role in Bahrain, where the Saudi and Bahraini monarchies have unjustly accused protesters of serving as agents of Iran, would deeply alarm Riyadh and Manama. There would also be a risk of more unilateral, aggressive and counterproductive Saudi measures to secure its interests by pre-empting what it would see as Iranian power grabs. For instance, it could further choke off the reform process in Bahrain and increase its security role there. Such an incorporation of Iran into regional security co-operation would also run the risk of weakening Western influence in those capitals.

For a host of reasons connected with energy interests, counter-terrorism, commerce and inertia, Western states cannot realistically dismiss the anxieties of their Gulf Arab allies. However, this does not mean uncritically accepting their policy positions. Tactical co-operation should be pursued where it can. In Afghanistan, where Iran has long played a key role in anti-Taliban coalitions, this will be especially important as Western forces draw down over the coming years. A dialogue with Iran on these areas is important, if only for the day when pragmatic factions re-emerge in the Iranian executive and once more come to dominate the leadership.

However, the central question is whether the cost of raising Iran's profile and perturbing longstanding allies is worth the medium- and longer-term gains that may be on offer, both in terms of eliciting a gradual change in Iranian foreign policy and, of relevance here, reducing Iran's incentive to seek nuclear weapons or the option of nuclear weapons. Iran's co-operative acts over the past fifteen years – such as Iran's reported support for the 2002 Saudi-led Arab peace plan for the Arab-Israeli conflict – are far less salient (and, of course, less frequent) than its competitive or subversive acts, but they are indicative of the possibility of détente, including in the nuclear realm, if not of something even more substantial.

---

[58] Haifa Zaaitar, 'Saudi Arabia, Iran Barred from Syria Conference', *Al-Monitor*, 29 June 2012.

Under ordinary circumstances, the United States and the West more broadly might have little need for détente with a politically and economically stagnant, middling regional power – but the nuclear backdrop, Israel's persistent military threats, and the impact of this crisis on the oil-dependent world economy all contribute to making this an undeniably special case. An unstable Iran, hollowed out by years of sanctions, facing the constant possibility of major war, and undergoing a crisis of political legitimacy is not conducive to stability in the Middle East. It is therefore in the long-term interests of all parties to ensure that this crisis does not become accepted as a permanent feature of the international system.

IV. THE IMPLICATIONS OF A NUCLEAR IRAN

As Iran's uranium stockpiles grow and diplomacy falters, the discourse around the nuclear crisis is growing both more apprehensive and more polarised. In this context, there has been a fresh series of warnings that a nuclear Iran would be more dangerous and costly than any plausible alternative. Even with strenuous and protracted diplomacy, and despite – or because of – a war with Iran, it is not beyond the realm of plausibility that Iran will obtain nuclear weapons. This would herald not the end of the crisis, but its mutation into a new and almost certainly more permanent form.

Many observers and policy-makers believe that such a new and intensified crisis is, literally, intolerable. In February 2012, thirty-two US senators from both parties introduced a non-binding resolution to rule out 'any policy that would rely on containment as an option in response to the Iranian nuclear threat'.[1] The following month, the US House of Representatives approved a resolution, with 314 sponsors, reiterating this message and that further specified 'the unacceptability of an Iran with nuclear-weapons *capability*' – that is, not just nuclear weapons, but even nuclear capabilities short of weaponisation.[2] In September 2012, President Obama did not go that far, but reiterated his earlier message that 'a nuclear-armed Iran is not a challenge that can be contained'.[3]

The assumption of these resolutions is that the cost of a nuclear Iran exceeds *any* cost whatsoever that might result from a policy of prevention through diplomatic or military means – including a full-scale war in the Gulf.

---

[1] Josh Rogin, '32 Senators Call for "No Containment" Strategy for Iran', *Foreign Policy: The Cable*, 16 February 2012.
[2] Howard LaFranchi, 'House Adopts Hard Line on Iran. Would Stance Move US Closer to War?', *Christian Science Monitor*, 17 May 2012. Emphasis added.
[3] Helene Cooper, 'Obama Tells U.N. New Democracies Need Free Speech', *New York Times*, 25 September 2012.

Concerns over the prospect of Iranian nuclear weapons is not confined to the US and Israel. British Foreign Secretary William Hague has warned of 'the most serious round of nuclear proliferation since nuclear weapons were invented', resulting in 'a new cold war in the Middle East' lacking all the 'safety mechanisms' of the US-Soviet rivalry.[4]

These and similar warnings typically rest on one, or all, of at least three distinct assumptions. First, that Iran is an irrational actor immune to the self-preservative logic of nuclear deterrence. Second, that a nuclear Iran or regional nuclear rivalry would present unprecedented challenges in terms of stability and safety. Third, that a nuclear Iran would precipitate an unstoppable chain reaction of regional nuclear proliferation. This section suggests that each of these assumptions reflects valid concerns that, through embellishment and imprecision, have resulted in overly simplistic understandings of the costs of a nuclear Iran.

Why does this analysis matter? In the past, even where the US has avowedly reasserted its non-proliferation aims – whether in relation to Israel, India, Pakistan or North Korea – it has eventually accepted a policy of containment rather than prevention or 'rollback' through military means. In May 2003, for instance, President Bush insisted that 'we will not tolerate nuclear weapons in North Korea. We will not give in to blackmail. We will not settle for anything less than the complete, verifiable and irreversible elimination of North Korea's nuclear weapons program'.[5] North Korea tested nuclear devices in 2006 and 2009. Iraq is a contradictory case, of course, insofar as American threats were sincere; but the prolonged and largely unsuccessful war in that country has reinforced Western caution in using force for non-proliferation objectives and has therefore made a war against Iran less likely.

The North Korea precedent alone indicates why it is important to develop our understanding of the implications of a nuclear Iran, both for Iran itself and for the region – even while acknowledging that such an outcome remains improbable.

Iran's Nuclear Options

Nuclear Posture
If Iran does decide to make one or, as would be more likely, more nuclear weapons, and successfully does so, it would then face a choice over its nuclear posture and doctrine. Nuclear posture refers to the 'capabilities, deployment patterns, and command and control procedures a state uses to

---

[4] *Daily Telegraph*, 'William Hague: A Nuclear Iran Could Cause a "Cold War"', 18 February 2012.
[5] *BBC News*, 'Stern Warning for N Korea', 23 May 2003.

manage and operationalize its nuclear weapons capabilities'.[6] Nuclear doctrine refers to the declaratory side of those operational arrangements, such as a state's articulated conditions for using nuclear weapons. In practice, posture and doctrine are interdependent, and may be considered together.

Roughly speaking, nuclear posture can vary along a spectrum from highly 'recessed' to highly 'ready'.

Examples of recessed postures include Pakistan in the late 1980s (said to be 'two screwdriver turns' away from bomb assembly), India in the 1990s, or South Africa in the 1980s. These states built nuclear weapons or created the option of doing so in a negligible amount of time, in some cases without directly testing their weapons. In South Africa's case, only six nuclear weapons were produced. These were stored unassembled in a vault, separately from their delivery systems, and under highly stringent political controls that made hair-trigger readiness impossible.[7]

A more 'ready' – but still relatively recessed – posture was chosen by India in the years after 1998. India's posture involved 'de-mating and dispersing its weapons components across civilian agencies ... to enhance their survivability and to establish a credible capability to retaliate against a nuclear strike'.[8] Indian scientists control the warheads and must hand them over to the military in a crisis.[9] Unlike South Africa, India has deployed its weapons; but it has done so with tight limits on the size, scope and readiness of the arsenal as a whole.

A third, more assertive posture is exemplified by Pakistan, which has developed a posture 'geared for the rapid (and asymmetric) first use of nuclear forces against conventional attacks to deter their outbreak, operationalizing nuclear weapons as usable warfighting instruments'.[10] Unlike the United States and Soviet Union during the Cold War, Pakistan does not intend or plan to launch a massive, disarming nuclear first strike on its opponents' nuclear forces. However, in contrast to India, Pakistan

[6] Vipin Narang, 'Posturing for Peace? Pakistan's Nuclear Postures and South Asian Stability', *International Security* (Vol. 34, No. 3, Winter 2010), p. 40.
[7] Peter Liberman, 'The Rise and Fall of the South African Bomb', *International Security* (Vol. 26, No. 2, Fall 2001).
[8] Narang, 'Posturing for Peace?', p. 46; Harsh V Pant, 'India's Nuclear Doctrine and Command Structure: Implications for Civil-Military Relations in India', *Armed Forces and Society* (Vol. 33, No. 2, January 2007); Ali Ahmed, 'Reviewing India's Nuclear Doctrine', Policy Brief, Institute for Defence Studies and Analysis, 24 April 2009; Rajesh M Basrur, *Minimum Deterrence and India's Nuclear Security* (Stanford, CA: Stanford University Press, 2006).
[9] Verghese Koithara, *Managing India's Nuclear Forces* (Washington, DC: Brookings Institution Press, 2012), p. 101.
[10] Narang, 'Posturing for Peace?', p. 46; Pant, 'India's Nuclear Doctrine and Command Structure'; Ahmed, 'Reviewing India's Nuclear Doctrine'; Basrur, *Minimum Deterrence and India's Nuclear Security*.

has placed less stringent limits on the size, diversity, readiness and target set of its arsenal.[11]

Posture is also related to the concept of 'opacity', referring primarily to the *discourse* around nuclear weapons, rather than their physical arrangements, and involving the non-acknowledgement of nuclear weapons, through secrecy, government censorship and self-censorship. Israel's nuclear arsenal offers the purest example of opacity.[12] On the one hand, certain nuclear postures do not allow for opacity. For example, one cannot openly and independently test a nuclear bomb whilst pretending not to have one. However, it is possible to have opaque arsenals that are both highly limited and highly advanced – indeed, Israel's arsenal has moved from the former to the latter, with only small concessions to transparency. Iran could similarly choose to build nuclear weapons and even deploy them, but publicly deny that it has done so.

This discussion of nuclear posture is, admittedly, an over-simplification. Nuclear postures vary along a number of dimensions other than readiness. These dimensions include: the threshold for use (for instance, whether as a response to nuclear attack or lesser regime-threatening actions); the targets of weapons (counterforce or countervalue); the role of weapons (perhaps war-fighting or signalling); the flexibility of response (ranging from massive retaliation to graduated deterrence); the delivery system (aircraft, missiles or naval platforms); and many others. There is an elective affinity between these dimensions (for example, a state that chooses a counterforce posture is likely to choose a larger arsenal) but they may exist in various combinations.[13]

---

[11] Narang, 'Posturing for Peace?', p. 44; Timothy D Hoyt, 'Pakistani Nuclear Doctrine and The Dangers of Strategic Myopia', *Asian Survey* (Vol. 41, No. 6, 2001); Scott D Sagan, 'The Evolution of Pakistani and Indian Nuclear Doctrine', in Scott D Sagan (ed.), *Inside Nuclear South Asia* (Stanford, CA: Stanford University Press, 2009).

[12] On how the principles of opacity may be relevant to a nuclear Iran, see Avner Cohen, *The Worst-Kept Secret: Israel's Bargain with the Bomb* (New York: Columbia University Press, 2010), Kindle edition, location 3469 (ch. 9).

[13] Note that a state may choose different positions along these different dimensions, even where this seems counterintuitive. It is possible to envisage a nuclear posture that accepts counterforce on the one hand but shuns nuclear war-fighting on the other. This would make sense if the military targets of counterforce were seen as valid targets for punishment rather than purely battlefield assets. An example of this can be found in aspects of Chinese nuclear thinking. See Alastair Iain Johnston, 'China's New "Old Thinking": The Concept of Limited Deterrence', *International Security* (Vol. 20, No. 3, Winter 1995–96), p. 19; M Taylor Fravel and Evan S Medeiros, 'China's Search for Assured Retaliation: The Evolution of Chinese Nuclear Strategy and Force Structure', *International Security* (Vol. 35, No. 2, Fall 2010), p. 70.

Why Does Posture Matter?
There are at least three reasons why nuclear posture matters. First, different postures can alter crisis dynamics. Should a crisis break out, for instance, Iran may have – or, more importantly, be *perceived* to have – more leverage if it has a dozen nuclear weapons deployed on missiles rather than a few unassembled warheads in storage.

Second, different postures may increase the risk of crises occurring in the first place. For example, if Iran were to deploy or threaten to deploy nuclear-armed missiles capable of striking European targets, this could prompt overt or covert attacks on Iranian missile sites, or a period of coercive diplomacy that induces a cycle of escalation.

Third, the response of regional powers, including their decisions whether or not to pursue nuclear capabilities of their own, is likely to depend on the nuclear posture chosen by Iran. If Iran shuns a nuclear test, refrains from declaring itself a nuclear power, and signals that its warheads would only be assembled in the event of a major threat to the state, this would likely meet with a different, more limited response than would the Iranian declaration of a deployed arsenal or a nuclear test. Iran's degree of nuclear opacity is likely to be particularly important in this regard.

Iran's Choice of Nuclear Posture
It must be considered, then, what sort of nuclear choices Iran might make should it acquire nuclear weapons. A number of factors would shape its choice.

First, states with civilian-dominated governments are loath to choose nuclear postures that empower and entrust their armed forces with such significant weaponry. For example, India's military in the 1990s, exceptionally subordinate to civilian institutions, had little idea of how many nuclear weapons India possessed or how they might be used in wartime (sealed instructions for nuclear use were given to a theatre commander, only to be opened in case of nuclear attack).[14] By contrast, military-dominated governments – like that of Pakistan – may, by virtue of the organisational preferences of the military as an institution, favour more assertive nuclear postures, and particularly postures that stress pre-emption and high degrees of readiness.[15]

In Iran, the pattern of nuclear decision-making remains unclear, even if the office of the supreme leader remains the most important locus of nuclear thinking.[16] The IAEA experienced difficulty 'in assigning

---

[14] Stephen Peter Rosen, *Societies and Military Power: India and Its Armies*, (Ithaca, NY: Cornell University Press, 1996), pp. 251–52.
[15] Scott D Sagan and Kenneth N Waltz, *The Spread of Nuclear Weapons: A Debate Renewed*, 2nd ed. (New York: W W Norton & Co, 2003), pp. 53–55.
[16] Nader Entessar, 'Iran's Nuclear Decision-Making Calculus', *Middle East Policy* (Vol. 16, No. 2, Summer 2009), pp. 31–34.

personal responsibility or authority for directing nuclear activities in Iran involving military-affiliated personnel and organizations – in particular the Iran Revolutionary Guard Corps'. Moreover, 'US officials have asserted again and again since the 1990s [that the IRGC] was responsible for key parts of Iran's nuclear program'.[17] Indeed, Mohsen Fakhrizadeh, an officer of the IRGC, was alleged to have led 'Project 111', Iran's pre-2003 covert nuclear-weapons programme identified in American and IAEA assessments.[18] The Pakistani nuclear scientist and proliferator A Q Khan has also implicated IRGC officials.[19]

Any crude comparison between Pakistan's praetorian political system, in which the military clearly sits above civilian actors, and Iran's hybrid system of pluralistic, factional competition should be treated with wariness. However, the IRGC has grown over the course of the 1990s to the point where it forms 'an expansive socio-political-economic conglomerate whose influence extends into virtually every corner of Iranian political life and society'.[20] This could contribute to tendencies away from a recessed deterrent towards more expansive postures.

This tendency would be strengthened were Iranian weaponisation to prompt changes in the nuclear posture of Israel and the United States, and were regional adversaries of Iran (notably Saudi Arabia) to develop nuclear weapons and themselves choose assertive postures.

There are also further incentives for Iran to choose a more assertive posture. In the past, such postures have historically been associated with more effective deterrence. Vipin Narang, a professor at MIT who has researched the causes and consequences of nuclear postures, draws lessons from South Asia to argue that 'evidence suggests that Pakistan's threat of early nuclear weapons use on Indian forces has had a significant inhibitory effect on India's political leadership', and that this threat was only credible *after* Pakistan shifted to an 'asymmetric escalation' nuclear posture.[21] By contrast, India's more relaxed posture has not stopped Pakistani-sponsored attacks on its soil. Nor have Israel's highly opaque nuclear weapons deterred multiple attacks on Israeli soil. The inference is that more aggressive postures seemingly offer better shields.

---

[17] Mark Hibbs, 'An IAEA Conversation with Rafsanjani', Arms Control Wonk blog, 18 October 2011.

[18] David E Sanger, 'U.S. Rejected Aid for Israeli Raid on Iranian Nuclear Site', *New York Times*, 10 January 2009; Mark Fitzpatrick, 'Assessing Iran's Nuclear Programme', *Survival* (Vol. 48, No. 3, Autumn 2006).

[19] R Jeffrey Smith and Joby Warrick, 'Pakistani Scientist Khan Describes Iranian Efforts to Buy Nuclear Bombs', *Washington Post*, 14 March 2010.

[20] Frederic Wehrey et al, *The Rise of the Pasdaran: Assessing the Domestic Roles of Iran's Islamic Revolutionary Guards Corps* (Santa Monica, CA: RAND Corporation, 2009), p. xi.

[21] Narang, 'Posturing for Peace?', p. 66.

Although it is argued later in this study that these lessons may be only partially applicable to the situation in the Gulf, Iranian leaders may nevertheless decide that only a deployed and ready arsenal will achieve the required deterrence, particularly in the face of the heightened security competition and pressure that would likely ensue in the aftermath of Iranian weaponisation.

Over time – towards the upper limit of the breakout timelines described in Chapter II – Iran would have the technological wherewithal to build a nuclear arsenal deployed on land-based missiles. Iran already has a variety of missile capabilities built around Russian, North Korean and Chinese technology. Taken together, Iran possesses the largest ballistic-missile inventory in the Middle East.[22] The most relevant missiles are the medium-range Shahab-3 and its variants. The Shahab-3, based on the North Korean No-dong-1, has a range of 1,000–1,500 km, which would cover targets ranging from Turkey to India and Ukraine to Yemen.

Iran is also developing longer-range variants, while the US Department of Defense has informed Congress that 'with sufficient foreign assistance, Iran could probably develop and test an intercontinental ballistic missile capable of reaching the United States by 2015'.[23] However, it should be noted that this date represents a highly unrealistic technical possibility, not a likelihood.[24]

At present, Iran's ballistic missiles are highly inaccurate, and thus contribute little to Iran's conventional capabilities.[25] Moreover, Iran's adversaries possess advanced theatre missile-defence systems. For instance, Saudi Arabia operates the Patriot Advanced Capability-2 (PAC-2) system, with approximately 800 interceptors for ballistic-missile defence. Assuming two interceptors are allocated to each incoming missile, as is standard, this would allow Saudi Arabia to target the first 400 missiles before exhausting its supply (which would anyway be replenished in any realistic conflict scenario). Assuming a 10 per cent success rate, based on the system's performance in the First Gulf War, Iran would need well over a 1,000 missiles just to achieve a 75 per cent chance of destroying any one tower at Saudi Arabia's key oil stabilisation facility at Abqaiq, which itself would cause only temporary delays in the flow of oil. Yet Iran is thought to

---

[22] Anthony H Cordesman and Abdullah Toukan, 'Analyzing the Impact of Preventive Strikes against Iran's Nuclear Facilities', Center for Strategic and International Studies, 10 September 2012, p. 45.
[23] Phil Stewart and Adam Entous, 'Iranian Missile May Be Able to Hit U.S. by 2015', *Reuters*, 19 April 2012.
[24] Jeffrey Lewis, 'Iranian ICBM by 2015?', Arms Control Wonk blog, 21 April 2010.
[25] Anthony H Cordesman and Alexander Wilner, 'Iran and the Gulf Military Balance II: The Missile and Nuclear Dimensions', Center for Strategic and International Studies, 16 July 2012, pp. 6–10.

have only around 400 missiles in its arsenal currently.[26] This inaccuracy would make little difference if the missiles had a nuclear payload.

It must be asked, therefore, how rapidly Iran is progressing in the development of missiles. In November 2011, a huge explosion occurred at a major Iranian missile-testing site, which is presumed to have set back the programme.[27] However, Iranian advances in solid-fuel technology and countermeasures to missile defence, as well as growth in the size and accuracy of its arsenal, will bolster Iran's ability to deploy a more survivable land-based, nuclear-missile force, if it so chooses in the future.

Incentives for Nuclear Restraint

Eric Edelman, Andrew Krepinevich and Evan Montgomery, researchers at the Center for Strategic and Budgetary Assessment in Washington, DC, declare confidently that 'Tehran would almost certainly attempt to expand the size of its arsenal to enhance the survivability of its nuclear weapons'.[28] Yet, despite the factors outlined above, Iran also faces incentives in the other direction, towards restraint.

First, Iran may judge that it can obtain at least two of the putative benefits of nuclear weapons – regional prestige and regime survival – without adopting an assertive nuclear posture, or perhaps even without overt weaponisation.

It has been argued that Iran looks to the divergent fates of (nuclear) North Korea and Pakistan on the one hand, and (non-nuclear) Saddam Hussein's Iraq and Muammar Qadhafi's Libya on the other.[29] If so, the North Korean case suggests that a reasonable degree of protection is afforded by the most rudimentary of weapons: indeed, 'Pyongyang showed that a nuclear arsenal does not have to be large or sophisticated to be politically effective'.[30] The United States perceives a constraint in its ability to coerce North Korea even though 'North Korea does not have operational missiles capable of striking the US with nuclear weapons, and will likely not be able to develop them as long as it continues its current moratorium on flight-testing'.[31] To be sure, this American inhibition is partially explained by, first, South Korea's unique vulnerability to North

---

[26] *Ibid.*, pp. 6–10.
[27] These calculations are drawn from Joshua R Itzkowitz Shifrinson and Miranda Priebe, 'A Crude Threat: The Limits of an Iranian Missile Campaign Against Saudi Arabian Oil', *International Security* (Vol. 36, No. 1, 2011), pp. 6–10.
[28] Eric S Edelman, Andrew F Krepinevich, Jr and Evan Braden Montgomery, 'The Dangers of a Nuclear Iran', *Foreign Affairs*, 1 January 2011, p. 68.
[29] Martin Indyk, 'Iran Spinning Out of Control', *New York Times*, 29 February 2012.
[30] Siegfried S Hecker, 'Lessons Learned from the North Korean Nuclear Crises', *Daedalus* (Vol. 139, No. 1, Winter 2010), p. 11.
[31] 'North Korea's Ballistic Missile Programme', *IISS Strategic Dossier*, 2004.

Korea's conventional retaliation and, second, China's diplomatic support to Pyongyang. However, even North Korea's basic nuclear status has bolstered the pre-existing North Korean retaliatory capacity. There is a risk that a small or non-deliverable Iranian arsenal might risk pre-emption rather than produce deterrence. Yet this has to be balanced against the more threatening nature of a larger and more deliverable arsenal. Iran could lessen this risk by heightening survivability, for instance through dispersal and ensuring that weaponisation could take place quickly.

Second, although a nuclear Iran would face tightened economic sanctions and political pressure anyway, a more assertive nuclear posture could invite even greater pressure. That would exacerbate Iran's already serious economic troubles. Iranian leaders may not wish to invest in a larger arsenal if they see the bomb primarily as a political rather than military weapon, particularly as a heavy nuclear burden would divert resources from other military priorities.

Third, Iran might not wish to give its non-nuclear rivals, like Saudi Arabia and Turkey, reasons for developing their own nuclear weapons. This incentivises both opacity and restraint. Iran's adversaries would be affected by *perceptions* of Iran's nuclear status, rather than the technical details *per se*.[32] An Iran that ostentatiously shows off its nuclear weapons is far more likely to induce a countervailing response than an Iran that quietly signals its nuclear status to decision-makers abroad without public fanfare. Iran would retain the option of simply denying that it possesses nuclear weapons, or adopting a similar rhetorical approach to Israel – promising not to be the first state to 'introduce' nuclear weapons to the region.

This would not be easy for Iran. It faces near-unprecedented scrutiny in its nuclear activities. Unlike US policy towards Pakistan in the 1980s, which was tempered by the need to co-operate with Pakistan in Afghanistan against the Soviet Union, the US and its allies today would be unlikely to withhold details of covert Iranian weaponisation. Nevertheless, opacity has never required perfect deniability. Israel's nuclear denials are widely understood as fictions. Yet, its policy allows both its allies (the United States) and adversaries (particularly Egypt) to collude in that fiction and limit their own responses, which might otherwise be necessarily more robust. Iranian opacity simply could not operate as smoothly, in part because there is no guarantee that others would collude in the fiction as they have done for Israel. Nonetheless, this possibility should not be dismissed out of hand.

What this indicates is that if Iran did actually put together a bomb, it might not be deployed or declared. Iran, a large country with substantial conventional strength, has strategic depth. It can wait for threats to develop

---

[32] See Dalia Dassa Kaye and Frederic M Wehrey, 'A Nuclear Iran: The Reactions of Neighbours', *Survival* (Vol. 49, No. 2, Summer 2007), p. 121.

rather than keeping weapons on hair-trigger alert. India, for a decade after its first nuclear test, did not even bother to prepare a bomb. When it eventually did, neither it nor Pakistan deployed their weapons for another ten years.[33]

Nuclear Fanaticism

As important as Iran's potential nuclear posture is how a nuclear-armed Iran would behave. The first argument, that Iran is an irrational actor that would not conform to the constraining logic of nuclear deterrence, is in keeping with a long tradition of imputing an unresponsiveness to deterrence to adversaries.[34] These arguments usually assess irrationality along various dimensions: a regime's willingness to accept risks; the ideological or theological content of its belief systems; the revisionist nature of its foreign policy; the degree of aggressive or apocalyptic rhetoric it employs; and so on.

Iran has been indicted on virtually all such counts. American columnist Charles Krauthammer has argued that Mahmoud Ahmadinejad is an 'aspiring genocidist, on the verge of acquiring weapons of the apocalypse, believes that the end is not only near' and would have 'less inhibition about starting Armageddon than a normal person. Indeed, with millennial bliss pending, he would have positive incentive to . . . hasten the end'.[35] In similar fashion, Aaron Goldstein, a writer at the *American Spectator*, suggests that 'it is not far-fetched to believe Iran is prepared to deploy a nuclear weapon against the only country in the world with a Jewish majority'.[36] Such views have found the greatest prominence in segments of the American and Israeli press, in part because of Jewish history.

Yet the notion that Iran's irrationality is unprecedented finds little support. Stalin's Soviet Union, which had absorbed over 20 million wartime deaths, sponsored politically subversive communist movements in Western Europe, and killed millions of its own citizens, was viewed in similarly threatening terms as Iran today. National Security Council Report 68 (commonly known as NSC-68), one of the formative statements of American foreign policy in the twentieth century, written just a year after the Soviet Union acquired nuclear weapons, judged Moscow to be

---

[33] Ashley J Tellis, *India's Emerging Nuclear Posture: Between Recessed Deterrent and Ready Arsenal* (Santa Monica, CA: RAND Corporation, 2001).

[34] John Mueller, *Atomic Obsession: Nuclear Alarmism from Hiroshima to Al Qaeda* (Oxford: Oxford University Press, 2010), ch. 5.

[35] Charles Krauthammer, 'In Iran, Arming for Armageddon', *Washington Post*, 16 December 2005.

[36] Aaron Goldstein, 'There is Nothing Rational about Iran's Regime', *American Spectator*, 13 March 2012.

'animated by a new fanatic faith, antithetical to our own', aimed at 'domination of the Eurasian landmass'.[37]

Western assessments of Mao Zedong's China were premised on a similar sense of menace. Tens of millions of peacetime deaths have been attributed to Mao's administration, including a great number during the period of the Great Leap Forward immediately preceding China's acquisition of nuclear weapons. Mao spoke in dismissive terms of nuclear war, arguing that 'imperialism would be razed to the ground, and the whole world would become socialist', and in generally belligerent terms that surpass Iranian rhetoric today.[38] Nonetheless, Mao adopted a highly restrained nuclear posture, one that remained vulnerable to a US or Soviet first strike for decades. That was not in spite of but *because* of Mao's personal view of nuclear weapons as instruments of retaliation, unfit for pursuing military objectives.[39]

These historical precedents are quickly forgotten in contemporary evaluations of a nuclear Iran. For example, Senator Joseph Lieberman's insistence in February 2012 that 'containment might have been viable for the Soviet Union during the Cold War, but it's not going to work with the current fanatical Islamist regime in Tehran'[40] is suspect. Former US Deputy Assistant Secretary of Defense Keith Payne argues likewise, and just as unpersuasively: 'we believed we had great insight into the thinking of the Soviet leadership, could communicate well with its officials, and that those leaders ultimately would behave in well-informed and predictable ways. Consequently, we could be wholly confident deterrence would "work". But today, there is no basis for comparable faith with regard to rogue regimes [like Iran]'.[41]

However, not only is it implausible to view Iran as qualitatively more fanatical than autocratic nuclear regimes of the past but, no less importantly, the nuclear behaviour of even these supposedly fanatical predecessors did not correspond to their belligerent rhetoric. Indeed, it is worth noting that Ahmadinejad – whose belligerent statements towards Israel are frequently adduced as evidence of Iranian irrationality – 'is actually ridiculed by many of his allies in the [IRGC] because of his apocalyptic rhetoric'.[42]

---

[37] US State Department, 'NSC 68: United States Objectives and Programs for National Security', 7 April 1950.

[38] Alan Lawrance, *China's Foreign Relations since 1949* (Abingdon: Taylor and Francis, 2007), p. 75.

[39] Fravel and Medeiros, 'China's Search for Assured Retaliation', p. 51.

[40] Rogin, '32 Senators Call for "No Containment" Strategy for Iran'.

[41] Cited in Francis J Gavin, 'Same as it Ever Was: Nuclear Alarmism, Proliferation, and the Cold War', *International Security* (Vol. 34, No. 3, Winter 2009–10), p. 14.

[42] Kaye and Wehrey, 'A Nuclear Iran', p. 124; for more detail, see Matthew Duss, 'The Martyr State Myth', *Foreign Policy*, 24 August 2011.

This more benign view of Iranian rationality is shared within important segments of the US government. In mid-February 2012, the Director of National Intelligence James Clapper told the Senate Armed Services Committee that any Iranian decision to build a nuclear weapon would be based 'on a cost-benefit analysis'. The then chief of the Defense Intelligence Agency Ronald Burgess stated that 'Iran is unlikely to initiate or intentionally provoke a conflict'.[43] This assessment flatly contradicts predictions that Iran would initiate nuclear conflict against Israel for messianic purposes.[44]

These comments were followed a week later by those from General Martin Dempsey, the chairman of the Joint Chiefs of Staff, that 'we are of the opinion that the Iranian regime is a rational actor'.[45] Meir Dagan, the former head of Israel's intelligence service, has also stated that Iran has 'a very rational regime', and that Ahmadinejad is himself 'rational', if 'not exactly our rational'.[46]

These assessments do not mean that Iran will necessarily abjure or behave cautiously with a bomb, but it implies a degree of reason that is at odds with contemporary alarmist accounts, and particularly with the periodic suggestions that Iran is likely unilaterally to use nuclear weapons to destroy Israel.[47]

There are, in fact, specific reasons why Iran is particularly vulnerable to robust deterrent threats that would dissuade any first strike. As Anthony Cordesman of the Center for Strategic and International Studies notes, 'the greater metropolitan area of Tehran is home to some 15 million people, which constitute 20 per cent of Iran's population. Furthermore, 45 per cent of large Iranian industrial firms are located in Tehran, as is 50 per cent of all Iranian industry'.[48] Some have also argued that Iran's vulnerability in this regard is exacerbated by Israel's overwhelming nuclear superiority, ensuring escalation dominance (that is, nuclear superiority at every plausible level of escalation in a crisis or conflict) over Iran, a state of affairs that will continue for decades, at least. This undercuts the argument that Iran, by virtue of being able to 'absorb' more nuclear bombs on its

---

[43] Ronald L Burgess, Jr, 'Statement Before the Senate Armed Services Committee', testimony on the current and future worldwide threats to the national security of the United States, 16 February 2012, available at <http://www.fas.org/irp/congress/2012_hr/021612burgess.pdf>, accessed 26 October 2012.

[44] Tom Wilson, 'Iran's Dangerous Concoction of Nuclear Ambitions and Shiite Messianism', *The Commentator*, 3 August 2011.

[45] Anna Mulrine, 'US Military Officials Urge Caution on Attacking Iran', *Christian Science Monitor*, 20 February 2012.

[46] *CBS News*, 'The Spymaster: Meir Dagan on Iran's Threat', 12 September 2012.

[47] Ian Deitch, 'Israeli Premier Says Iran Wants to Destroy Israel', *Associated Press*, 21 May 2012.

[48] Anthony H Cordesman, 'Iran's Evolving Threat', Center for Strategic and International Studies, 21 January 2010.

larger territory, would be able to gain relative advantage in a nuclear war. The versatility of Israeli nuclear options also mitigates the risk that Tel Aviv would be morally inhibited from retaliating against Iranian civilians on such a scale, because it could instead choose to engage in relatively more precise and discriminate targeting.

In private, Israeli officials place less emphasis on Iranian nuclear use and more on the broader effects. A leaked 2007 diplomatic cable from the US embassy in Tel Aviv stated that:[49]

> Israeli analysts point out that even if a nuclear-armed Iran did not immediately launch a strike on the Israeli heartland, the very fact that Iran possesses nuclear weapons would completely transform the Middle East strategic environment in ways that would make Israel's long-term survival as a democratic Jewish state increasingly problematic. That concern is most intensively reflected in open talk by those who say they do not want their children and grandchildren growing up in an Israel threatened by a nuclear-armed Iran.

If this statement refers to Israeli emigration prompted by an Iranian nuclear weapon, it is not borne out by the evidence. A 2009 poll from a respected Israeli think tank found that 'Israelis do not seem consumed by the Iranian nuclear threat. When asked how their personal lives might be affected by Iran acquiring nuclear weapons, 80 per cent stated that their lives would not change. Nine per cent said they would move to another community, 8 per cent would consider moving to another country, and only 3 per cent stated they would definitely emigrate from Israel'.[50] This is not a trivial figure, but it must be considered in the context of larger demographic changes in Israel, such as rising ultra-Orthodox fertility and a convergence in the fertility rates of Arab and Jewish Israelis.[51] Perhaps another reason for Israelis' sanguinity is that, according to the same poll, '79 per cent of Israeli Jews do not believe that Iran would attack Israel with nuclear weapons'.[52]

---

[49] *Guardian*, 'US Embassy Cables: Israeli Optimism Erodes in Face of Regional Enemies', 28 November 2010.

[50] Yehuda Ben Meir and Olena Bagno-Moldavsky, *Vox Populi: Trends in Israeli Public Opinion on National Security 2004-2009*, Memorandum No. 106 (Tel Aviv: Institute for National Security Studies, 2010), p. 25. However, nuclear weapons in the hands of Iran were viewed as the most serious threat facing Israel, measured at 6.2 on a 1–7 point scale.

[51] Jack A Goldstone, Eric P Kaufmann and Monica Duffy Toft, *Political Demography: How Population Changes are Reshaping International Security and National Politics* (Oxford: Oxford University Press, 2012), pp. 216–32.

[52] Ben Meir and Bagno-Moldavsky, *Vox Populi*, p. 24.

Crises, Brinkmanship and Instability

Brinkmanship

However, there is a second and more plausible set of concerns that nuclear weapons can rationalise the taking of dangerous risks.

Each side in a nuclear rivalry will fear escalation. At the same time, each side will be aware that its adversary is similarly afraid, and that excessive fear will permit the adversary the freedom to do as it pleases. As the historian Marc Trachtenberg puts it, 'a political dispute can [therefore] become a gigantic poker game, with each side raising the stakes in the hope that its opponent, frightened by the prospect of nuclear war, will fold before things go too far'.[53]

The very process of raising these stakes creates uncertainty. The pioneer of game theory, Thomas Schelling, conceptualised 'the threat that leaves something to chance'. The key to such threats is that 'though one may or may not carry them out if the threatened party fails to comply, the final decision is not altogether under the threatener's control' because of the possibility of inadvertent escalation. As such, this produces a 'threat to expose the other party, together with one's self, to a heightened risk of general war'. Schelling draws from this a definition of brinkmanship:[54]

> [T]he brink is not, in this view, the sharp edge of a cliff where one can stand firmly, look down, and decide whether or not to plunge. The brink is a curved slope that one can stand on with some risk of slipping, the slope gets steeper and the risk of slipping greater as one moves toward the chasm . . . Brinkmanship is thus the deliberate creation of a recognizable risk of war, a risk that one does not completely control. It is the *tactic of deliberately letting the situation get somewhat out of hand*, just because its being out of hand may be intolerable to the other party and force his accommodation.

The lesson for nuclear strategy is that between two nuclear states, the more reckless state should be able to stand at the brink for longer and thus end a crisis on its own terms. It follows that even if Iran were not irrational in absolute terms, even *relative* irrationality, being more irrational than an adversary, would offer some benefit in a crisis.

Whether a nuclear Iran would take greater risks, and the manner in which that would affect its foreign policy and constrain Western

---

[53] Marc Trachtenberg, 'Proliferation Revisited', University of California at Los Angeles, 24 June 2002, p. 4, <www.sscnet.ucla.edu/polisci/faculty/trachtenberg/cv/prolif.doc>, accessed 26 October 2012.
[54] Thomas C Schelling, *The Strategy of Conflict* (Cambridge, MA: Harvard University Press, 1960), pp. 188–91, 199–200. Emphasis added.

policy options, is a complex question that requires some exploration. The analysis below looks at the data on nuclear weapons and instability, and asks whether Iran would conform to these patterns. Then it considers in more detail how nuclear weapons might affect regional stability.

Empirical Evidence on Nuclear Weapons and Instability

A range of studies have asked how nuclear weapons affect behaviour. Michael Horowitz finds that 'when a nuclear asymmetry exists between two states [that is, where one state possesses nuclear weapons and the other does not], there is a greater chance of militarized disputes and war. In contrast, when there is symmetry and both states possess nuclear weapons, then the odds of war precipitously drop'.[55] The implication of this is that a nuclear Iran would have fewer disputes with Israel, but more with its non-nuclear regional adversaries.

Erik Gartzke and Dong-Joon Jo come to a conclusion along similar lines: 'nuclear weapons increase diplomatic status without much affecting whether states fight'.[56] Likewise, Kyle Beardsley and Victor Asal find that 'nuclear weapons . . . have little effect on overall crisis occurrence'.[57]

James Fearon of Stanford University also analyses how nuclear weapons have affected individual states' propensity to get involved in militarised disputes.[58] He finds that 'China, France, India, Israel, Pakistan, and the UK all saw declines in their total militarized dispute involvement in the years after they got nuclear weapons. A number of these are big declines'. This may be the result of non-nuclear factors, such as the process of decolonisation and European integration; but it might also be the case that nuclear-armed states are challenged less often, feel less compelled to join allies' fights, and are less prone to starting disputes for fear of escalation. The only exceptions to this pattern are Russia and South Africa.

---

[55] Michael Horowitz, 'The Spread of Nuclear Weapons and International Conflict: Does Experience Matter?', *Journal of Conflict Resolution* (Vol. 53, No. 2, April 2009).

[56] Erik Gartzke and Dong-Joon Jo, 'Bargaining, Nuclear Proliferation, and Interstate Disputes', *Journal of Conflict Resolution* (Vol. 53, No. 2, April 2009).

[57] Kyle Beardsley and Victor Asal, 'Nuclear Weapons as Shields', *Conflict Management and Peace Science* (Vol. 26, No. 3, July 2009).

[58] According to the Correlates of War project, militarised disputes refer to conflicts between states that do not involve a full-scale war. Such conflicts must cause fewer than 1,000 deaths, and some form of military force must be used or threatened. This definition is the standard one used in the field of political science. See Faten Ghosn, Glenn Palmer and Stuart Bremer, 'The MID3 Data Set, 1993–2001: Procedures, Coding Rules, and Description', *Conflict Management and Peace Science* (Vol. 21, 2004), pp. 133–54.

In quantitative terms, 'states see on average about one half fewer disputes per year when they have nuclear weapons' than when they do not.[59]

Even with the 'hard cases' of supposedly fanatical states, this pattern seems to hold. Francis Gavin demonstrates that 'nuclear weapons did not make China more hostile. If anything, its foreign policies became less aggressive and more mature over time'.[60]

Lessons from South Asia

A crucial exception to this pattern can be found in the literature on South Asia, in which many scholars have argued that Pakistan, after acquiring and testing nuclear weapons, grew emboldened to engage in limited aggression and offer greater assistance and protection to anti-Indian jihadist groups.

The usual explanation for this drew on what Glenn Snyder called the 'stability-instability paradox', whereby 'the Soviets probably feel, considering the massive retaliation threat alone, that there is a range of minor ventures which they can undertake with impunity, despite the objective existence of some probability of retaliation'.[61]

In the context of South Asia, this was interpreted as meaning that Pakistan, sitting behind a nuclear shield, could needle India in the knowledge that it would be inhibited from retaliating for fear of escalation to the nuclear level.[62] As Michael Krepon argues, 'Pakistan's active support for separatism and militancy in Kashmir has notably coincided with its acquisition of covert nuclear capabilities. Tensions between India and Pakistan have intensified further since both nations tested nuclear weapons in 1998'.[63]

Although this is not the only interpretation of South Asian nuclear dynamics – others argue that nuclear threats have in fact played little role in inhibiting India or emboldening Pakistan[64] – it does represent a potentially important and troubling precedent for Iranian behaviour.

---

[59] James Fearon, 'How do States Act after They Get Nuclear Weapons?', The Monkey Cage blog, 29 January 2012.
[60] Gavin, 'Same as it Ever Was', p. 10.
[61] Glenn H Snyder, *Deterrence and Defense: Toward a Theory of National Security* (Princeton, NJ: Princeton University Press, 1961), p. 226.
[62] S Paul Kapur, 'India and Pakistan's Unstable Peace: Why Nuclear South Asia is not Like Cold War Europe', *International Security* (Vol. 30, No. 2, Fall 2005), p. 146.
[63] Michael Krepon, 'The Stability-Instability Paradox, Misperception, and Escalation Control in South Asia', Henry L Stimson Center, May 2003, p. 2.
[64] Bharat Karnad, *India's Nuclear Policy* (Westport, CT: Praeger, 2008); Sumit Ganguly, 'Nuclear Stability in South Asia', *International Security* (Vol. 33, No. 2, Fall 2008); Peter R Lavoy (ed.), *Asymmetric Warfare in South Asia: The Causes and Consequences of the Kargil Conflict* (Cambridge: Cambridge University Press, 2009), pp. 10–12.

Iran, like Pakistan, deems its ties to non-state armed groups to be a significant part of its national security strategy.[65] As Michael Eisenstadt observes, 'the use of street mobs and violent pressure groups as instruments of domestic politics is an old tradition in Iran, going back at least to the Qajar dynasty'.[66] Although Iran is not the only state to use non-state proxy groups as parts of its policy – the US and Israel, for instance, have both adopted similar policies against Iran and elsewhere – the central role of proxy actors in Iranian strategic culture and its way of war should be recognised.

However, some of the inferences drawn from the experience of India and Pakistan may be misleading.

One crucial but almost wholly neglected distinction is that Pakistan hosts militants on its own soil, whereas Iran largely, though not exclusively, helps those 'off-site', in locations such as Lebanon and Palestine.[67] India faces potentially prohibitive costs in targeting, say, Lashkar-e-Taiba, because it would have to attack Pakistani territory to do so. In that scenario, Pakistani nuclear threats would likely be credible (although, as described earlier, this may also be a function of Pakistan's specific nuclear posture). Even limited Indian air strikes, limited enough to avoid meeting with a nuclear response from Pakistan, nonetheless run the risk of rapid escalation to a scenario in which such a response *is* credible.[68] Israel, by contrast, will continue to be able to strike at Hizbullah or Hamas on Lebanese or Palestinian soil *regardless* of Iran's nuclear status. Attacking the territory of a third party is quite different to, and therefore 'safer' than, attacking Iranian soil; for Israel will simply not believe that Iran will use nuclear weapons in response to an attack not directly targeting its own soil.

Iran could theoretically announce that its nuclear weapons henceforth covered Lebanon, and that attacks against Hizbullah would meet with the same response as if they were attacks on Tehran. Yet this attempt at extended deterrence would simply not be credible. Iran has historically demonstrated little sign of incurring major costs, let alone costs on the scale of Israeli nuclear retaliation, on behalf of its non-state allies and proxies in the past, prompting the question, therefore, why Iran would put Tehran at risk for the sake of southern Lebanon.

---

[65] Daniel Byman, 'Passive Sponsors of Terrorism', *Survival* (Vol. 47, No. 4, Winter 2005/06); Daniel Byman, *Deadly Connections: States that Sponsor Terrorism* (Cambridge: Cambridge University Press, 2005).

[66] Michael Eisenstadt, *The Strategic Culture of the Islamic Republic of Iran: Operational and Policy Implications* (Quantico, VA: Marine Corps University, August 2011), p. 7.

[67] Daniel Byman, 'Iran, Terrorism, and Weapons of Mass Destruction', *Studies in Conflict and Terrorism* (Vol. 31, No. 3, March 2008).

[68] Manoj Joshi, 'We Lack the Military That Can Deter Terrorism', *Mail Today*, 26 November 2009.

Although the US risked its own territory during the Cold War to put a nuclear umbrella over its European allies, the nature of those alliances differed. Whereas the 'loss' of a US ally might have resulted in the full industrial powers of that ally being turned against the Western alliance, the 'loss' of an Iranian ally is less damaging to Iran. After all, even if Hizbullah or Hamas were to lose their dominant positions in their respective territories, Iran would still retain influence, perhaps through alliances with different groups. Iran undoubtedly has expansive regional aspirations and in Syria it has shown a willingness to assist beleaguered allies. Under circumstances of grave Iranian vulnerability, Tehran might be tempted to take greater risks in assisting regional allies; but the extent of its support is likely to be limited.

Would Iran consider deploying nuclear forces on the territory of its allies? The Soviet Union sent missiles to Cuba to redress its perceived strategic inferiority against the United States. Yet Iran's placement of missiles in Lebanon rather than Iran would not give it a comparable leap in reach. More importantly, Iranian interests are simply not commensurate with the immense risks.[69]

An important consideration here is whether Iran's allies could exploit an Iranian nuclear weapon. Jean-Loup Samaan suggests that 'Hizbullah . . . could play the game of "calculated irrationality": in the midst of a conflict, an emotional, out-of control declaration from Hassan Nasrallah threatening nuclear retaliation could convey the intended impression of irrationality that would deter the Israeli Defense Forces'.[70] However, such a statement would likely be treated with derision, not fear. It would be as if Slobodan Milosevic had threatened NATO with Russian nuclear attack during the Kosovo War of 1999. Only if Iran made a concerted effort to extend deterrence over Hizbullah would such a declaration carry weight – but this means returning to the question of why Iran would take risks so disproportionate to its interests.

The Continued Relevance of Limited War

Possession of nuclear weapons would, at the very least, enable Iran to deter attacks on its 'core' territory. This limits the options of its adversaries. However, even though Iran has been persistently associated with deadly attacks on Western forces in Iraq and Afghanistan in recent years, through the provision of lethal assistance to non-state armed groups in those countries, large-scale ground attacks on Iran itself have never been viewed

---

[69] Paul Pillar, 'We Can Live with a Nuclear Iran', *Washington Monthly* (March/April 2012).
[70] Jean-Loup Samaan, 'The Day after Iran Goes Nuclear: Implications for NATO', Research Paper No. 71, NATO Defense College, January 2012, p. 5.

as a credible or desirable retaliatory option. What has been and would remain credible in dealing with a nuclear-armed Iran is the use of force on different targets and at lower levels of force. One example of this would be Operation *Praying Mantis*, the US attack on Iranian naval forces in 1988.[71]

Limited war remains possible under nuclear conditions, despite the risks that attend it.[72] Understanding the parameters of limited war – what remains possible under a nuclear overhang – represents the greatest intellectual and practical challenge for policy-makers who may have to come to grips with a nuclear Iran.

It is worth returning to South Asia for an illustration, where both India and the United States have engaged in limited uses of force against nuclear-armed Pakistan. In 1999, India militarily responded to Pakistan's invasion of Kashmir's Kargil sector, despite the mutual possession of nuclear weapons. India carefully restricted attacks to its own side of the Line of Control, even though this placed India's infantry forces at severe tactical disadvantage and increased casualties.[73] In subsequent years, India developed a conventional army doctrine that envisions the use of territorially limited ground assaults in response to Pakistani or Pakistan-linked aggression.[74] Pakistan's nuclear weapons have also failed to deter American and Afghan special forces raids into Pakistani territory in recent years.[75]

In these cases, the crucial point is that Pakistani nuclear threats would not have been credible. In the case of Kargil, India successfully remained below Pakistan's nuclear threshold. It could therefore apply its greater military strength. The conventional balance proved decisive, despite both sides' possession of nuclear weaponry.

Turning to how this experience can be applied to Iran, it is clear that in the Gulf the conventional balance is, and will remain, unkind to Iran (see Figure 2). In 2010, Iran's defence expenditure comprised 10.56 per cent of the regional total, whereas Saudi Arabia's comprised 45.17 per cent, Israel 17.17 per cent, and the UAE 8.65 per cent. In 2011, Iran's proportion of regional spending fell to less than 10 per cent. By

---

[71] Patrick Knapp, 'The Gulf States in the Shadow of Iran: Iranian Ambitions', *Middle East Quarterly* (Vol. 17, No. 1, Winter 2010).
[72] Lawrence Freedman, *The Evolution of Nuclear Strategy*, 3rd ed. (Basingstoke: Palgrave Macmillan, 2003), pp. 93–100.
[73] Peter R Lavoy, 'Why Kargil Did Not Produce General War: The Crisis Management Strategies of Pakistan, India, and the United States', in Peter R Lavoy (ed.), *Asymmetric Warfare in South Asia*, p. 192.
[74] Walter C Ladwig III, 'A Cold Start for Hot Wars? The Indian Army's New Limited War Doctrine', *International Security* (Vol. 32, No. 3, Winter 2007/08).
[75] Shashank Joshi, 'A Very Special Relationship: The US-Pakistan Alliance Darkens', *RUSI.org*, 26 September 2011.

Figure 2: Comparative regional defence spending, 2000–08 (total spend, 2010 dollars).

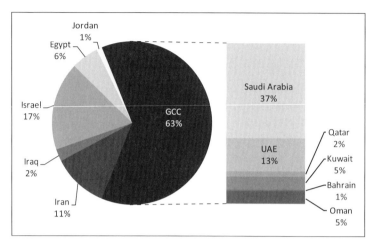

Source: Data adapted from SIPRI.

comparison, the spending of the GCC states *excluding Saudi Arabia*, comprises 17 per cent of the total. Including Saudi Arabia, that figure rises to 54.3 per cent.[76] These figures underplay the asymmetric threat from Iran's navy and missile forces, but they also exclude the near-certain involvement of the United States in any major regional crisis. In short, the military superiority of Iran's adversaries over Iran far exceeds that of India's over Pakistan in 1999. That superiority strictly limits what Iran can achieve, because nuclear threats would only be credible in a very narrow range of scenarios.

The question of credibility of nuclear threats is therefore an important one, because a limited war with Iran would present different challenges depending on, first, the issue under consideration – that is, the location of any crisis – and, second, Iran's particular nuclear posture. A more aggressive nuclear posture might, as with the case of Pakistan, render Iranian threats more credible.

Crises closer to Iran's borders may also present greater challenges, as the risk of escalation to the point of threatening core Iranian territory would be greater, thus rendering any Iranian nuclear threats more credible, and in turn limiting the feasible boundaries of the use of force against Iran. If Iranian-backed militants were to seek shelter on Iranian soil, this would

---

[76] International Institute for Strategic Studies, *The Military Balance* (Vol. 112, No. 1, 2012), p. 306.

be the most difficult scenario of all, because it would parallel the Indian dilemma *vis-à-vis* Pakistan.

This means that Iranian aggression in, say, neighbouring Iraq might incur less risk and therefore may well become easier, because Iranian soil, protected by nuclear weapons, would become a safer location from which to undertake such action: 'Iran could seek to initiate disputes over the extraction of oil and gas reserves, funnel assistance to Shiite extremists, and engage in plausibly deniable terrorist attacks' in the region,[77] all with a greater sense of impunity.

However, the marginal advantage that such an Iranian policy would add to its present, advantageous position in Iraq is questionable. Moreover, there would be no US or allied inhibition whatsoever regarding striking Iranian forces on Iraqi soil. Of course, deniable proxy actors are, by their nature, hard to target using conventional military means.

This relates to the question of whether Iran could leverage its nuclear status to secure concessions from its neighbours. Ash Jain, of the Washington Institute for Near East Policy, argues that Gulf States would 'accommodate and appease Tehran' should Iran acquire nuclear weapons.[78] However, in considering how Iran might apply this pressure, it is insufficient to suggest, as Jain does, that Iran would simply 'initiate disputes'. If Iran threatened or used force, there is no reason why commensurate retaliatory threats could not be made and, if necessary, carried out – as long as these were limited and, perhaps, as long as the US could successfully offer some form of reassurance to the threatened state or states in question.

Nuclear coercion against non-nuclear states is in fact much harder to implement than is assumed. If this were not so, the UK would have had little trouble in employing nuclear coercion to expel Argentina from the Falklands Islands, and the US would have had little trouble in expelling the Soviet Union from Eastern Europe during the years of its nuclear monopoly in the early Cold War. In both cases, the conventional balance (and perceptions thereof) proved to be extremely important.

Nevertheless, it is important to consider the implications should Iran directly use its own forces to pressure other states. Jean-Loup Samaan, of NATO's Defense College, argues that 'even in a scenario in which the Israeli Defense Forces had evidence that Iran was supporting Hizbullah's adventurism, they would have to refrain from directly attacking Iranian targets and limit the scope of any retaliation to Hizbullah targets in order to avoid uncontrolled escalation'.[79] Yet Indian forces in Kargil had no trouble

---

[77] Ash Jain, 'Nuclear Weapons and Iran's Global Ambitions: Troubling Scenarios', Policy Focus No. 114, Washington Institute for Near East Policy, August 2011, p. ix.
[78] *Ibid.*
[79] Samaan, 'The Day after Iran Goes Nuclear', p. 5.

attacking Pakistani forces dressed as mujahedeen, despite Pakistan's possession of nuclear weapons. Similarly, Israel could hit (and kill) Soviet forces, including high-ranking officers, present in Egypt during the 1973 war, despite the USSR's possession of nuclear weapons.[80] Therefore, it is unclear why Israel would refrain from striking Iranian targets in Lebanon.

If Iran chose to escalate on the territory of a third party by sending more forces, it would almost certainly be at a serious conventional disadvantage. If Iran escalated using conventional stand-off capabilities, such as missiles launched from Iranian soil, these might indeed enjoy a certain protection or immunity, depending on their firing location. However, their low accuracy would produce a limited effect on the battlefield, and only for a limited time. Such a step would also symbolically legitimate retaliation in kind, into Iranian territory, and that retaliation would be both more precise and more durable than anything Iran could achieve. It is important not to be sanguine about the risk-acceptance that this form of escalation requires; however, too often the leap is made from the (reasonable) notion that risk exists to the (untenable) conclusion that its inhibitory effects will be crippling to one side alone.

There are also other factors that further distinguish Iran from Pakistan, and suggest why it would be easier for Iran's adversaries to retaliate against Iran than it has been for India to retaliate against Pakistan. Pakistan can credibly depict even limited war with India as a potential threat to the existence of the Pakistani state. This is because Pakistan is a narrow country, and its cities and interior transport links are near vulnerable borders. By contrast, Iran is a large country with its key population centres and capital away from sensitive borders. If the United States or Israel were to launch air strikes on outlying parts of Iran, this would be a qualitatively different act to Indian ground offensives over the Punjabi border. This is because the former would be intrinsically less threatening to Iran's survival as a state.

Additionally, the use of stand-off capabilities, such as air strikes, is different in kind to India's policy options. This is because there is a clear, sharp line between stand-off strikes and land warfare. With India and Pakistan, there is no such dividing line, principally because of the contiguity of the two countries, but also because of the historical precedent of the dismemberment of Pakistan in 1971. Any Indian punitive action against Pakistan unavoidably generates a crisis in which ground forces come into play, even if only as a result of Pakistani initiation. In other words, the escalatory potential of any conventional Indian action is greater, and therefore the use of force more plausibly existential in

---

[80] Bruce D Porter, *The USSR in Third World Conflicts: Soviet Arms and Diplomacy in Local Wars 1945–1980* (Cambridge: Cambridge University Press, 1986), p. 135.

nature than would be the case for other countries. Pakistani nuclear threats are therefore more proportionate in nature. In nuclear deterrence, proportionality matters in terms of credibility. By contrast, American or Israeli action against Iran can occur without such forces coming into play. This mitigates, though does not eliminate, the risk of rapid escalation, because it allows force to be used in a way that is limited, is mutually *understood* to be limited, and can more easily be *signalled* as limited.

Of course, this logic would not hold if Tehran itself were attacked, or if a large American ground force mobilised on Iran's borders. In that situation, Iranian nuclear threats would certainly be credible. Moreover, there is no easy distinction between peripheral and non-peripheral interests. Iran's adversaries could misperceive Iran's definition of its core interests, perhaps by escalating gradually and inadvertently blurring the line between peripheral and core interests. Iran, conversely, could overestimate the defensive power of nuclear weapons, and thereby take risky steps that precipitate a war. Misperception of where the boundary lies can be extraordinarily dangerous in the nuclear context.

In the final instance, it is impossible to predict the degree to which a nuclear Iran's adversaries would be inhibited from potentially escalatory actions. They may be considerably more inhibited than is suggested here, which would indeed strengthen Tehran's hand. Certainly, the sanctity of core Iranian territory would preclude forcible regime change. As the political scientist Kenneth Waltz notes, 'if a country has nuclear weapons, it will not be attacked militarily in ways that threaten its manifestly vital interests. That is 100 per cent true, without exception, over a period of more than fifty years'.[81] Even if a range of military options remained viable, these would be more limited than what had been possible before Iran became a nuclear-armed state. With such protection, Iran might be willing to take risks that it previously was not, even allowing for the prospect and likelihood of retaliatory action. Moreover, those limits would be ambiguous and Iran, like other nuclear states, would presumably work hard to keep them as ambiguous as possible in ways that blurred the risk calculation for adversaries. Should war break out, it would carry with it objectively greater risks owing to the role of brinkmanship, or competitive risk-taking. Each side would be forced to explore and experiment with the range of coercive options at its disposal, from the use of proxy forces to ballistic missiles, without fully comprehending the other side's reaction. Miscalculation during such a process could lead to uncontrollable escalation.

---

[81] Scott Sagan, Kenneth Waltz and Richard K Betts, 'A Nuclear Iran: Promoting Stability or Courting Nuclear Disaster', *Journal of International Affairs* (Vol. 60, No. 2, 2007), p. 137.

Iranian Prestige

The dynamics above refer to how nuclear weapons affect crises and conflict. However, a nuclear Iran may also affect the more general balance of power and prestige in the Middle East, independently of any concrete change in Iran's coercive powers.[82] Iran has longstanding aspirations to regional leadership, out of proportion with its economic or military power. It is possible that nuclear weapons, especially if openly deployed, would strengthen these aspirations on symbolic grounds alone, make other regional states more amenable to this narrative, and lessen the influence of the United States in the region.[83]

Richard Russell, for instance, suggests that 'the Saudis probably would suffer a sense of political humiliation that the Iranians have the political prestige or reputation for power that accompanies nuclear weapons', with the implication that a reputation for power can, in turn, translate into real power.[84] In turn, Avner Cohen writes that 'even if Iran never actually dropped a bomb on Israel, a nuclear-capable Iran would destroy Israel's sense of vitality and self-confidence'.[85]

Arguments about the prestige of a nuclear Iran are difficult to assess. If prestige is purely symbolic and has no further effect, it has few security implications for Western or other states. If it does, however, enhance Iranian leverage, then that would be a greater challenge – although such leverage is more likely to flow from a perception of Iranian immunity than it is from prestige *per se*.

In the case of North Korea and Pakistan, their acquisition of nuclear weapons has not substantially increased their prestige; in fact, both are perceived as irresponsible nuclear stewards.[86] Although their vulnerability to foreign pressure has probably lessened in certain ways, this has come about despite a *loss* of prestige, not because of an *increase* in it.

Furthermore, although India has successfully leveraged its nuclear status to secure certain exemptions from the non-proliferation regime, this route would be no more open to Iran than it has been to Pakistan. India, once a pariah in the nuclear order itself, is perceived as a rising power with a history of responsible nuclear and foreign-policy behaviour. Iran, by

---

[82] For an example of this argument, see F Gregory Gause III, *Oil Monarchies: Domestic and Security Challenges in the Arab Gulf States* (New York: Council on Foreign Relations, 1994), p. 169.

[83] Jain, 'Nuclear Weapons and Iran's Global Ambitions', p. xi.

[84] Richard L Russell, 'Arab Security Responses to a Nuclear-Ready Iran', in Henry Sokolski and Patrick Clawson (eds), *Getting Ready for a Nuclear-Ready Iran* (Carlisle, PA: Strategic Studies Institute, US Army War College, 2005), p. 31.

[85] Cohen, *The Worst-Kept Secret*, Kindle edition, location 217 (Introduction).

[86] *Daily Telegraph*, 'North Korea Ranked Last on Nuclear Safety – Australia First', 11 January 2012; Jeffrey Goldberg and Marc Ambinder, 'The Ally From Hell', *Atlantic Monthly*, December 2011.

contrast, is a stagnating autocracy perceived as a malign regional force. In other words, it is unlikely that withdrawal from or violation of the NPT, and the acquisition of nuclear weapons, would in fact increase Iranian prestige, or that any such increase would alter Iran's ability to secure favourable outcomes.

Multipolar Deterrence

The second set of arguments concerns multipolar deterrence. The likelihood and nature of second-order nuclear proliferation caused by Iranian weaponisation is examined later in this section. However, the effects of any such proliferation on deterrence and crisis stability ought to be considered here.

A nuclear Iran would leave three states possessing nuclear weapons in the Middle East: Israel, Iran and, through extended deterrence, the United States. Although the latter is an extra-regional power, the mobility and reach of its forces, along with its local basing arrangements and strong presence in the region, means that it should be understood as a regional nuclear power, too. Similarly, the UK and France might also claim that, with their regional basing and alliances, and expeditionary capabilities, they, too, should fall under this category. Further proliferation could then create new nuclear states, including Saudi Arabia, Egypt, Turkey and others. Finally, a nuclear Iran could eventually possess the capability to strike at continental European targets, and at states which presently consider Iran an adversary. They, too, will consider themselves part of a further nuclearised Middle East.

Deterrence amongst more than two powers is not an entirely new challenge. During the Cold War, British, French and Chinese nuclear forces all impinged on the US-Soviet relationship in different ways.[87] Chinese nuclear weapons were particularly challenging, as they existed in a triangular relationship with US and Soviet weapons wherein every set of weapons potentially targeted the other (whereas French and British weapons targeted neither each other nor American forces).

Multipolar nuclear deterrence, or 'multipolar nuclear interactions',[88] are challenging for at least two reasons.

Attribution

First, nuclear deterrence depends on attribution. Only by *accurately* attributing a nuclear strike to a single, deterrable entity can we hope to

---

[87] James C Wendt and Peter A Wilson, *Post INF: Toward Multipolar Deterrence* (Santa Monica, CA: RAND Corporation, 1988), pp. 23–27.
[88] Gavin, 'Same as it Ever Was', p. 10.

make our deterrent threats credible. When there are multiple nuclear entities, such a process of attribution grows more difficult. According to a recently declassified intelligence assessment from 1984, 'the existence of the separately controlled US, British, and French strategic nuclear strike systems increase[d] Moscow's uncertainty about nuclear escalation'.[89] This was not only because it was unclear which Soviet adversaries might participate in a retaliatory strike, but also because it would not always be clear which ones might have launched a first strike – particularly from submarines (it is notable that the US, too, had doubts over its ability to make such distinctions).[90]

The existence of separately controlled US and Israeli nuclear weapons therefore presents a challenge for Iran. Separately controlled Iranian and, say, Saudi Arabian nuclear weapons would generate similar problems for the US, Israel and Europe – and perhaps even Pakistan and India. The problem would worsen if India were in the future to deploy nuclear-armed submarines in the region.

This problem is especially acute for three further reasons: first, the proximity of these states and the correspondingly short missile and, to a lesser extent, aircraft flight times;[91] second, the lack of sophisticated early-warning systems that could compensate for such short flight times; and third, the possession and deployment of dual-use ballistic missiles – that is, those capable of carrying both conventional and nuclear warheads. Each of these problems is a feature of the scenario in South Asia, where missile flight times are a matter of a few minutes.[92] However, they assume greater prominence in a multipolar setting in which identifying the source of a nuclear strike may not be simple.

---

[89]   US Intelligence Community, 'Warning of War in Europe', 1984, p. 24, available at <http://www.foia.cia.gov/docs/DOC_0001486834/DOC_0001486834.pdf>, accessed 26 October 2012.
[90]   William A Owens, Kenneth W Dam and Herbert S Lin, *Technology, Policy, Law, and Ethics Regarding U.S. Acquisition and Use of Cyberattack Capabilities* (Washington, DC: National Academies Press, 2009), p. 294; Glenn C Buchan, David M Matonick, Calvin Shipbaugh and Richard Mesic, *Future Roles of U.S. Nuclear Forces: Implications for U.S. Strategy* (Santa Monica, CA: RAND Corporation, 2003), p. 15; Sam Nunn, 'Changing Threats in the Post-Cold War World', in John M Shields and William C Potter (eds), *Dismantling the Cold War: U.S. and NIS Perspectives on the Nunn-Lugar Cooperative Threat Reduction Program* (Cambridge, MA: MIT Press, 1997), p. xiv.
[91]   Edelman, Krepinevich, Jr and Montgomery, 'The Dangers of a Nuclear Iran', p. 74; Anthony H Cordesman and Khalid R Al-Rodhan, *Gulf Military Forces in an Era of Asymmetric Wars* (Westport, CT: Greenwood, 2007), p. 221.
[92]   Rajesh M Basrur, *South Asia's Cold War: Nuclear Weapons and Conflict in Comparative Perspective* (Abingdon: Routledge, 2008), p. 68.

Calculating Sufficiency and Vulnerability

Second, multipolar nuclear relationships can complicate a state's calculations about the survivability and sufficiency of its own nuclear arsenal. States might resort to worst-case calculations and develop arsenals based on the aggregate nuclear capability of any plausible coalition of nuclear states ranged against them. Moreover, efforts to configure a deterrent to a number of different states is difficult, and increases the probability of error. As Christopher Ford observes, 'the more players there are, the more chances there will be for the system to break down, through accident, error, miscalculation, miscommunication, or some other pathology'.[93]

Safety and Security Mechanisms

The second argument concerning the prohibitive cost of Iranian nuclear capabilities encompasses safety and security – not just that of an Iranian arsenal, but also that relating to broader nuclear rivalries that might develop as a result. Nuclear safety refers to the risks of accidents involving nuclear materials, while nuclear security refers to risks of acquisition of nuclear materials by unauthorised actors.

Scott Sagan of Stanford University argues that the covert, military-run and resource-starved nuclear programmes of emerging nuclear powers can result in poor safeguards on fissile material and on the weapons themselves.[94] The extent to which such arguments apply to a nuclear Iran will depend on a number of factors, of which Iran's choice of nuclear posture will be the most important. A highly recessed nuclear posture, like that of South Africa, is far safer in terms of securing weapons from unauthorised or accidental launch than a highly assertive posture, like that of Pakistan.

In Pakistan's case, 'it is believed that single or proximate military bases store all the necessary components for rapid assembly and deployment in a crisis', probably 'at military locations in a tight, elongated band toward the rear of Punjab and Sindh, south of Islamabad'. Moreover, 'there may be few safeguards that physically prevent lower-level officers from taking each step without authorization if they deem it necessary, as a hedge if the [Nuclear Command Authority] is out of reach or decapitated'.[95]

---

[93] Christopher Ford, 'Thinking About a Poly-Nuclear Middle East', Hudson Institute, 9 July 2012.
[94] Sagan and Waltz, *The Spread of Nuclear Weapons*, pp. 73–74; Sagan, Waltz and Betts, 'A Nuclear Iran', pp. 141–42.
[95] Narang, 'Posturing for Peace?', pp. 66–68.

These measures all stem from Pakistan's choice of posture. By contrast, and as discussed earlier, there are reasons to suppose that a nuclear Iran may not choose to implement such measures. (Indeed, Pakistan itself did not do so for a decade after weaponising.) For instance, as a result of its greater strategic depth, Iran is less concerned about being militarily overrun and losing its nuclear weapons. It is more insulated from the 'use or lose' dilemma perceived by Pakistan (though not immune to it, given the precision strike capabilities of both Israel and the United States).

Yet whatever posture it chooses, Iran will face similar choices to other nuclear states: whether to opt for safety through secrecy and opacity (making it vulnerable to insider threats during, say, transportation) or through prominent physical protection (making it vulnerable to major military attack on visible, fixed locations, unless these are deeply buried). If a nascent Iranian nuclear arsenal is subject to military threats, or if Iranian nuclear stewards perceive such threats, they may respond by moving their nuclear forces (or just their warheads) frequently and covertly to prevent the location of those assets becoming known. Military threats against small and vulnerable arsenals are not unknown, and will likely exacerbate existing safety problems.[96]

Pakistan is an example of a state that has opted for secrecy as part of its protection measures, with tight control and compartmentalisation of information pertaining to nuclear materials.[97] However, that same secrecy requires low-profile security, which raises the vulnerability of nuclear materials *if* their location becomes known.[98]

We should temper these concerns with the understanding that Iran faces a very different threat environment to Pakistan. Pakistan has a 'permissive environment for violent, non-state actors'.[99] Iran does not. In addition, the apex body for nuclear decision-making would, barring dramatic changes in the structure of the Iranian state, be the office of the supreme leader, a civilian-clerical body, which has more control and influence over its armed forces, and would therefore likely demand better control over nuclear weapons, than Pakistani civilians.[100] (Of course, one

---

[96] Sagan and Waltz, *The Spread of Nuclear Weapons*, pp. 63–65; Matthew Fuhrmann and Sarah E Kreps, 'Targeting Nuclear Programs in War and Peace: A Quantitative Empirical Analysis, 1941–2000', *Journal of Conflict Resolution* (Vol. 54, No. 6, December 2010).

[97] Christopher Clary, 'Thinking about Pakistan's Nuclear Security in Peacetime, Crisis and War', Occasional Paper No. 12, Institute for Defence Studies and Analyses, New Delhi, September 2010, p. 13.

[98] Narang, 'Posturing for Peace?', pp. 72–73.

[99] Clary, 'Thinking about Pakistan's Nuclear Security', p. 21.

[100] Peter Jones, 'Succession and the Supreme Leader in Iran', *Survival* (Vol. 53, No. 6, 2011/12), p. 106.

might argue that an Iranian civilian is no less risk-averse than a Pakistani general.)

Nonetheless, there is a paradox of safety: Iranian weaponisation is likely to result in a period of greatly heightened tensions, in which the focus will be on coercing rather than engaging with Iran. However, that is a formative period in which Iran could make consequential decisions about the scope and scale of the nuclear forces it will eventually build. More importantly, other small nuclear states, like Pakistan, have received substantial assistance, in the form of hundreds of millions of dollars, from the United States in securing their nuclear weapons.[101] It is unrealistic to expect the US to provide Iran with assistance, not only because that might be perceived as a legitimisation of those weapons' development, but also because the US domestic political environment, and the US Congress in particular, would almost certainly be hostile to such a development.

The discussion so far has considered nuclear safety *within* a nuclear Iran. A separate area concerns nuclear safety *between* Iran and other nuclear states. Here, a further lesson from the Indo-Pakistan rivalry is useful. These two countries have defied William Hague's suggestion of February 2012, made in reference to Iran, that emerging nuclear powers are incapable of implementing safety mechanisms.[102]

For instance, in the same week that Hague issued this warning, India and Pakistan extended for another five years an earlier nuclear-safety pact on reducing the risks from accidents related to nuclear weapons.[103] The pact, which first came into effect in 2007, obliges each country to improve the security and safety of its own nuclear arsenal, inform the other of any nuclear accident, and take steps to minimise cross-border effects of any such accident. In the previous month (January 2012), India and Pakistan had exchanged the lists of their nuclear installations for the twentieth consecutive year, under an agreement that prohibits any kind of attack on such facilities.[104] That agreement was originally reached in 1985, long before the states weaponised as such, but it was formalised in 1998.[105] During the 1999 Lahore summit, a large number of substantial nuclear

---

[101] David E Sanger and William J Broad, 'U.S. Secretly Aids Pakistan in Guarding Nuclear Arms', *New York Times*, 18 November 2007.
[102] *Daily Telegraph*, 'William Hague: A Nuclear Iran Could Cause a "Cold War"', 19 February 2012.
[103] *The Hindu*, 'India, Pak Agree to Extend Nuclear Risk Reduction Pact for 5 Years', 21 February 2012.
[104] *The Hindu*, 'India, Pakistan Exchange Nuclear Lists', 1 January 2012.
[105] George Perkovich, *India's Nuclear Bomb: The Impact on Global Proliferation* (Berkeley and Los Angeles, CA: University of California Press, 2001), p. 276.

confidence-building measures was agreed by both sides – such as an agreement to notify the other party of ballistic-missile tests.[106] These agreements have endured despite the outbreak of war, multiple crises (after the 2001 attack on India's parliament, and after the 2008 Mumbai attack – both of Pakistani provenance), and changes of government and regime type in Pakistan.

It is important to avoid a fatalistic policy approach that, on the basis of Western concerns over Middle Eastern nuclear instability, brings about through passivity the circumstances it fears. Iran, through its aggressive actions, has persistently weakened the assumptions and institutions on which ordinary diplomatic exchange depends. Any process of weaponisation would strain trust and generate pressures to isolate Iran further. Yet the concerns over nuclear safety, documented above, require *more* communication and not less. The Israeli, American, Saudi Arabian and other Arab governments will be understandably loath to initiate such discussions for fear of giving Iran the diplomatic status it seeks or of indicating even tacit approval of a nuclear Iran. However, the possible scope of these nuclear safety mechanisms between Iran and other present or future nuclear powers needs to be explored today, and not left until after such a scenario comes about.

Second-Order Nuclear Proliferation

Apart from the implications for Iranian behaviour, a nuclear Iran is feared for what it may engender in terms of further nuclear proliferation, and the resultant 'possibility of a highly unstable regional nuclear arms race'.[107] If Iranian weaponisation might be considered 'first-order proliferation',[108] then these further rounds of nuclear-weapons acquisition might be termed 'second-order proliferation'.[109]

Saudi Arabia, Egypt and Turkey are the three states with the most obvious motive and opportunity to pursue nuclear weapons themselves in response to any Iranian weaponisation, thereby constituting second-order proliferation. Weaponisation might also have an impact on the nuclear postures of existing nuclear-armed states, including – in order of probable impact – Israel, the United States, Pakistan, Russia and India. Weaker,

---

[106] Bhumitra Chakma (ed.), *The Politics of Nuclear Weapons in South Asia* (Farnham: Ashgate Publishing, 2011), pp. 204–05.
[107] Edelman, Krepinevich, Jr and Montgomery, 'The Dangers of a Nuclear Iran', p. 67.
[108] Obviously, this is to set aside Israeli nuclear weapons – which, in any case, have not been a motive force behind Iran's nuclear activities.
[109] The phrase is used in Bruno Tertrais, 'The Consequences for NATO of a Nuclear-Armed Iran', Halifax Paper Series, German Marshall Fund of the United States, 1 November 2010.

poorer and smaller states are likely to have lower incentives and fewer means of acquiring nuclear weapons.

Factors Affecting Second-Order Proliferation

When considering non-nuclear states' decisions over whether to pursue nuclear weapons, it is useful to evaluate five separate factors – the first of which applies in general, and the other four to each state individually. This list is not exhaustive; some factors, like public opinion regarding nuclear weapons, are not considered in detail. (The term 'triggering state' is used here to denote the state whose weaponisation has 'initiated' the putative cascade, while 'proliferation candidate' is used to describe the state(s) considering a response. In this study, the triggering state under consideration is obviously Iran.)

1. Nuclear posture: how recessed or assertive, and opaque or transparent, is the nuclear posture of the triggering state?
2. Threat perception: how antagonistic is the proliferation candidate's existing relationship to the triggering state?
3. Nuclear capabilities: what are the proliferation candidate's means, whether indigenous or foreign, of acquiring the fissile material and technology necessary for nuclear weapons?
4. Security guarantees: what are the proliferation candidate's alternative means for acquiring nuclear protection – for instance, through placing itself under the US nuclear umbrella – and what faith does it have in such means?
5. Broader security: how would the pursuit of nuclear weapons affect the proliferation candidate's broader security? What diplomatic and other costs would result from proliferating, and how well equipped is the candidate to resist these costs?

Taken together, these factors suggest that there is a real risk of second-order proliferation in the Middle East, with Saudi Arabia characterised by the greatest risk. However, it is important to remember both that, first, empirically, nuclear proliferation has not historically been as self-perpetuating as has been forecast, claimed or assumed; and second, there are strong, and potentially decisive, *disincentives* to acquire nuclear weapons, as well as incentives, and that some of these are subject to manipulation through the policy levers of those Western governments ostensibly most concerned about nuclear proliferation.

Proliferation Alarmism

The historical record suggests that nuclear weapons do not inevitably, or even usually, beget nuclear weapons. Most intelligence estimates over the years have drastically overstated the number of countries likely to obtain bombs. A declassified American document from 1964, the year of China's first nuclear test, highlighted 'at least eleven nations (India, Japan, Israel, Sweden, West Germany, Italy, Canada, Czechoslovakia, East Germany, Romania, and Yugoslavia) with the capacity to go nuclear', with 'South Africa, the United Arab Republic, Spain, Brazil and Mexico' to follow.[110]

Of these states, only India, Israel and South Africa in fact went on to obtain nuclear weapons, with only two continuing to possess them today. Other states on this list – like Sweden and Brazil – initiated nuclear-weapons programmes but later abandoned them.[111] Others still – like Japan – are not known to have had nuclear-weapons programmes, but maintained a high degree of nuclear latency, such that it would not take very long to design and fabricate deliverable nuclear weapons.[112]

Clearly, proliferation trends have been far less rapid than expected – whether because of the restraining effect of the global non-proliferation regime (including the NPT and its *accoutrements*) or other factors, such as the declining managerial competency in would-be proliferators.[113] Moeed Yusuf, of the United States Institute for Peace, argued that 'the pace of proliferation has been consistently slower than has been anticipated by most experts due to a combination of overwhelming alarmism, the intent of threshold states, and many incentives to abstain from weapons development' – the latter two factors being potentially crucial in the case of both Iran and its adversaries.[114] Francis Gavin, in his overview of proliferation alarmism, goes as far as to suggest that 'no nation has *started* a new nuclear weapons program since the demise of the Soviet Union in 1991'.[115]

---

[110] Cited in Francis J Gavin, 'Blasts from the Past: Proliferation Lessons from the 1960s', *International Security* (Vol. 29, No. 3, Winter 2004/05), p. 17.

[111] Wolfgang K H Panofsky, 'Capability versus Intent: The Latent Threat of Nuclear Proliferation', *Bulletin of the Atomic Scientists*, 14 June 2007.

[112] Scott D Sagan, 'Nuclear Latency and Nuclear Proliferation', in William C Potter and Gaukhar Mukhatzhanova (eds), *Forecasting Nuclear Proliferation in the 21st Century, Vol. 1: The Role of Theory* (Stanford, CA: Stanford University Press, 2010), p. 98; Llewelyn Hughes, 'Why Japan Will Not Go Nuclear (Yet): International and Domestic Constraints on the Nuclearization of Japan', *International Security* (Vol. 31, No. 4, Spring 2007); Jacques E C Hymans, 'Veto Players, Nuclear Energy, and Nonproliferation: Domestic Institutional Barriers to a Japanese Bomb', *International Security* (Vol. 36, No. 2, Fall 2011).

[113] Jacques E C Hymans, 'Botching the Bomb: Why Nuclear Weapons Programs Often Fail on Their Own – and Why Iran's Might, Too', *Foreign Affairs* (May/June 2012).

[114] Moeed Yusuf, 'Predicting Proliferation: The History of the Future of Nuclear Weapons', Policy Paper No. 11, Brookings Institution, January 2009, p. 4.

[115] Gavin, 'Blasts from the Past', p. 19. Emphasis added.

In particular, certain proliferation 'domino effects' between rival states that might have been thought inevitable simply never transpired. When the Soviet Union obtained the bomb, Yugoslavia and Sweden – the former a state that was to break with Moscow in particularly bitter fashion and that therefore had every reason to fear Soviet intentions – did not have security guarantees.[116] However, neither followed with the acquisition of nuclear weapons (although both preserved a nuclear option for a time).[117] Neither did Taiwan follow China, even after the US-China rapprochement after 1971 reduced the credibility of its external security guarantees.[118] Furthermore, South Korea followed neither China nor, later, North Korea.[119]

It might be argued that all of these states, Yugoslavia excepted, were allies, clients or informal partners of the United States, and that they therefore enjoyed an additional layer of conventional and, in some cases, nuclear protection from their nuclear adversaries. Yet this is also true of Iran's rivals today: Saudi Arabia and Egypt are longstanding allies of the United States and major recipients of military assistance, and Turkey is a fully fledged member of NATO, a nuclear alliance.

One final point is worth considering. India tested a nuclear device in 1974 but did not weaponise until the late 1980s, and did not do so overtly (with a test) until 1998.[120] Despite a hostile relationship with China that persisted into the late 1980s, India did *not* choose to follow Beijing's weaponisation. When India eventually did so, it was prompted as much by domestic political factors, concerns over shifts in the global non-proliferation regime, and anxiety over the conventional (rather than nuclear) balance as it was by the nuclear status of its rival.[121] There was no direct and proximate relationship between China's weaponisation and

---

[116] This was true at least until 1960, when the US did offer some guarantees to Sweden. See S Moores, '"Neutral on Our Side": US Policy towards Sweden during the Eisenhower Administration', *Cold War History* (Vol. 2, No. 3, April 2002), p. 50.

[117] See, respectively, Gaukhar Mukhatzhanova, 'Nuclear Weapons in the Balkans: Why Yugoslavia Tried and Serbia Will Not', in Potter and Mukhatzhanova (eds), *Forecasting Nuclear Proliferation in the 21st Century*; T B Johansson, 'Sweden's Abortive Nuclear Weapons Project', *Bulletin of the Atomic Scientists* (Vol. 42, No. 3, March 1986).

[118] David Albright and Corey Gay, 'Taiwan: Nuclear Nightmare Averted', *Bulletin of the Atomic Scientists* (Vol. 54, No. 1, January/February 1998).

[119] Christopher W Hughes, 'North Korea's Nuclear Weapons: Implications for the Nuclear Ambitions of Japan, South Korea, and Taiwan', *Asia Policy* (Vol. 3, January 2007), pp. 96–98.

[120] Perkovich, *India's Nuclear Bomb*, p. 317.

[121] Sumit Ganguly, 'India's Pathway to Pokhran II: The Prospects and Sources of New Delhi's Nuclear Weapons Program', *International Security* (Vol. 23, No. 4, Spring 1999).

that of India. A similar dynamic is evident in the other 'shadow dominoes' discussed above.

This historic trend of excess pessimism regarding proliferation ought to be kept in view when assessing the proliferation risks presented by the countries below.

Saudi Arabia

Regional powers fear Iran and the prospect of an Iranian nuclear weapon. However, they do so to highly varying degrees. Saudi Arabia's fears are probably the most acute of any proliferation candidate, for reasons laid out at length earlier in this study. It is reasonable to assume that Saudi Arabia will view Iranian weaponisation as a major threat to the security, prestige and interests of the Kingdom and its allies. Moreover, Saudi Arabia's ability to acquire a nuclear weapon exceeds that of any other relevant state, and its faith in external security guarantees is perhaps the most tenuous. For these reasons, Saudi Arabia's role in any proliferation cascade ought to be considered the most credible.

Saudi Arabia is a member of the NPT. Although it possesses some nuclear infrastructure such as a nuclear research centre dating to 1975, and civil nuclear agreements with China, France, South Korea and Argentina, 'the Kingdom does not appear to possess the necessary technical infrastructure to develop [a nuclear weapon] indigenously, bar significant infusions of external assistance'.[122]

However, Riyadh's reported role in funding the Pakistani nuclear programme likely provides it with just that assistance, and therefore the ability to procure fissile material; the technology and equipment to produce fissile material, including centrifuges; the technology for weapons design; a nuclear weapon itself; the use of Pakistani nuclear weapons stationed on Saudi soil; or some combination thereof. There is little publicly available evidence for this nuclear relationship, but officials who would have been privy to such evidence in their formal roles suggest that it is a valid inference. Brice Riedel, a former senior CIA analyst and presidential adviser, explicitly writes that the two states 'today have an unacknowledged nuclear partnership to provide the kingdom with a nuclear deterrent on short notice if ever needed'.[123] Neither Riedel nor other former officials have provided evidence for such a partnership, however.

---

[122] Wyn Q Bowen and Joanna Kidd, 'The Nuclear Capabilities and Ambitions of Iran's Neighbors', in Sokolski and Clawson (eds), *Getting Ready for a Nuclear-Ready Iran*, p. 53.
[123] Bruce Riedel, 'Saudi Arabia: Nervously Watching Pakistan', Brookings Institution, 28 January 2008.

Nevertheless, Saudi Arabia and Pakistan have a long history of security co-operation. Pakistan helped the Royal Saudi Air Force to build and pilot its first jet fighters in the 1960s, and Pakistani personnel flew Saudi aircraft during a Yemeni cross-border war in 1969.[124] In subsequent decades, as many as 15,000 Pakistani troops were stationed in Saudi Arabia, 'some in a brigade combat force near the Israeli-Jordanian-Saudi border'.[125] In 1986, Pakistan's Saudi presence comprised one division (roughly 13,000 troops), two armoured and two artillery brigades (approximately 10,000 troops), along with naval and air force personnel.[126] Pakistani forces reportedly 'fill[ed] out most of the 12th Saudi Armored Brigade' based at Tabuk.[127] This brigade reportedly left in 1988, after Saudi Arabia demanded that Pakistan send only Sunni personnel.[128] It is unclear how many Pakistani personnel remain in Saudi Arabia, but Pakistan does provide assistance and personnel to Bahrain, which is a de facto protectorate of Saudi Arabia, and to other GCC members.[129]

This Saudi-Pakistan security co-operation has almost certainly had a nuclear dimension. In the 1970s, Pakistani Prime Minister Zulfikar Ali Bhutto reportedly sought and received Saudi Arabian assistance in bankrolling Islamabad's nuclear programme. As Ian Talbot, a historian of Pakistan, observes, 'Arab money (Libyan and Saudi) was vital for Bhutto's quest to secure a Pakistani bomb'.[130] Furthermore, Robert Baer, a former CIA officer, has put a figure of $1 billion on Saudi funding, although he supplies no source.[131]

---

[124] Nadav Safran, *Saudi Arabia: The Ceaseless Quest for Security* (Ithaca, NY: Cornell University Press, 1988), p. 202.

[125] Riedel, 'Saudi Arabia'.

[126] C Christine Fair, 'Has the Pakistan Army Islamized? What the Data Suggest', Working Paper 2011–13, Mortara Center for International Studies, Edmund A Walsh School of Foreign Service, Georgetown University, September 2011, pp. 19–20.

[127] Anthony H Cordesman, *Western Strategic Interests in Saudi Arabia* (London: Taylor and Francis, 1987), p. 139.

[128] C Christine Fair, *Pakistan: Can the United States Secure an Insecure State?* (Santa Monica, CA: RAND Corporation, 2010), p. 121. Thomas Lippman claims that the forces left because 'oil prices hit historic lows and the Saudis could no longer afford them'; see Thomas W Lippman, 'Nuclear Weapons and Saudi Strategy', Middle East Institute Policy Brief No. 5, January 2008, p. 8.

[129] Mujib Mashal, 'Pakistani Troops Aid Bahrain's Crackdown', *Al Jazeera*, 30 July 2011.

[130] Ian Talbot, *Pakistan: A Modern History* (New York: St Martin's Press, 1998), p. 238; Gordon Corera, *Shopping for Bombs: Nuclear Proliferation, Global Insecurity, and the Rise and Fall of the A.Q. Khan Network* (Oxford: Oxford University Press, 2009), p. 13.

[131] Robert Baer, *Sleeping with the Devil: How Washington Sold Our Soul for Saudi Crude* (New York: Three Rivers Press, 2003), p. 35.

In 1998, when Pakistan was considering whether and when to respond to India's nuclear tests, Saudi Arabia offered a supply of oil to insulate Pakistan from the costs of its decision. According to one account, 'For three years after the 1998 nuclear tests Pakistan did not have to pay for the oil that it was provided by Saudi Arabia'.[132] SIPRI estimates that the support amounted to 150,000 barrels of oil per day.[133]

In 1999, Saudi Defence Minister (and later Crown Prince) Prince Sultan visited Pakistan for an unprecedented tour of nuclear facilities. There, he met with Pakistan's preeminent nuclear scientist, A Q Khan, who was later implicated in the most serious nuclear black market activities in proliferation history.[134] US officials, citing 'a lack of clarity by Saudi Arabia when Washington asked why the minister had visited the plants, one for uranium enrichment at Kahuta and one for missiles', were deeply alarmed at the visit.[135] A Q Khan himself would visit Saudi Arabia that same year, and again in 2000.[136]

In 2002, the son of then-Crown Prince (now King) Abdullah attended a test-firing of Pakistan's medium-range, nuclear-capable Ghauri missile. Immediately after that visit, the *Washington Times*, citing a 'ranking Pakistani insider', reported that Saudi Arabia and Pakistan 'have concluded a secret agreement on nuclear cooperation that will provide the Saudis with nuclear-weapons technology in exchange for cheap oil'.[137] Such reports have been common. In February 2012, *The Times* reported that:[138]

> In the event of a successful Iranian nuclear test, Riyadh would immediately launch a twin-track nuclear weapons programme, The Times has learnt. Warheads would be purchased off the shelf from abroad, with work on a new ballistic missile platform getting under way to build an immediate deterrent, according to Saudi sources. At the same time, the kingdom would upgrade its planned civil nuclear programme to include a military dimension, beginning uranium enrichment to develop weapons-grade material in the long term.

---

[132] Aparna Pande, *Explaining Pakistan's Foreign Policy: Escaping India* (Abingdon: Routledge, 2011), p. 156.

[133] Yana Feldman, 'Saudi Arabia: Past Nuclear Policies', SIPRI, July 2004.

[134] Adrian Levy and Catherine Scott-Clark, *Deception: Pakistan, the United States, and the Secret Trade in Nuclear Weapons* (New York: Walker Publishing Company, pp. 286–87.

[135] Jane Perlez, 'Saudi's Visit to Arms Site in Pakistan Worries U.S.', *New York Times*, 10 July 1999.

[136] Mark Fitzpatrick (ed.), 'Nuclear Black Markets: Pakistan, A.Q. Khan and the Rise of Proliferation Networks', *IISS Strategic Dossier*, 2007, p. 83.

[137] *Washington Times*, 'Pakistan, Saudi Arabia in Secret Nuke Pact', 21 October 2003.

[138] Hugh Tomlinson, 'Saudi Arabia Threatens to Go Nuclear "Within Weeks" if Iran Gets the Bomb', *The Times,* 10 February 2012.

These reports are typically ambiguous as to the precise nature of this nuclear co-operation, but most assume that Saudi Arabia would purchase warheads. In 1994, a defecting Saudi diplomat, seeking political asylum in the United States, claimed that Saudi Arabia had tried to purchase nuclear research reactors from China and from a US company in 1989, with the intention of producing fissile material for weapons.[139] However, an indigenous enrichment or reprocessing programme, even one 'jump-started' with Pakistani (or, more improbably, Chinese) assistance, would be a far more difficult endeavour than more direct forms of weaponisation.

Saudi Arabian policy need not depend upon the simple purchase of a warhead, as is sometimes assumed. Nuclear *sharing* rather than nuclear *transfer*, an arrangement akin to that practised by the US with its NATO allies, might be an equally workable and more legally sound option for both countries. Recall that, by the end of the 1950s, around 500 nuclear weapons were deployed to non-US NATO forces. In many cases, these allowed for 'independent European launch' and in 1959, President Eisenhower admitted that 'we are willing to give, to all intents and purposes, control of the weapons. We retain titular possession only'.[140]

As Jean-Loup Samaan points out, 'nothing, in theory, would legally prevent [Pakistani-Saudi nuclear sharing] as long as these weapons are not under the control of the recipient country . . . Pakistan is not a party to the Non-Proliferation Treaty and, in this scenario, the Saudi interpretation of articles I and II of the NPT would be similar to the US interpretation, unchanged since the late 1960s'.[141] These are the two articles of the NPT that prohibit signatories (including Saudi Arabia) from any transfer or receipt of nuclear weapons or assistance to that end. Since the late 1960s at least, the US has held to the legal position that, first, these injunctions do not cover nuclear-capable *delivery systems*, which *can* be legally transferred and received, and, second, that the NPT 'would no longer be controlling' when 'a decision were made to go to war' (which is known as the 'wartime exclusion' or 'exception').[142]

It is not hard to imagine Saudi Arabia proffering a similar rationale. It would be difficult to quibble with the legality, given that NATO's own

---

[139] Paul Lewis, 'Defector Says Saudis Sought Nuclear Arms', *New York Times*, 7 August 1994.
[140] Marc Trachtenberg, *A Constructed Peace: The Making of the European Settlement, 1945–1963* (Princeton, NJ: Princeton University Press, 1999), pp. 193–200.
[141] Samaan, 'The Day after Iran Goes Nuclear', p. 6; see also Richard L Russell, 'A Saudi Nuclear Option?', *Survival* (Vol. 43, No. 2, 2001).
[142] Martin Butcher, Ottfried Nassauer, Tanya Padberg and Dan Plesch, *Questions of Command and Control: NATO, Nuclear Sharing and the NPT*, PENN Research Report 2000, Project on European Nuclear Non-Proliferation, Berlin, March 2000, pp. 21–22.

nuclear-sharing agreements are under particular scrutiny today.[143] Pakistan could also offer nuclear guarantees *without* nuclear sharing, or even without stationing nuclear forces on Saudi soil: as Bruno Tertrais observes, 'ballistic missiles based in south-western Pakistan would have the range to cover a significant portion of the Saudi neighbourhood'.[144] This, however, would raise problems of credibility, particularly given Pakistan's vulnerability to Iranian missiles as a result of the two states' proximity.

Furthermore, Saudi Arabia is the only major proliferation candidate to possess viable delivery systems for any future nuclear warheads. In 1986, Saudi Arabia purchased between fifty and sixty CSS-2 intermediate-range ballistic missiles from China after the US refused to sell missiles capable of hitting Israel.[145]

Riyadh's claim that, despite these missiles' nuclear-capable origins, they had been modified by China to carry conventional payloads only are contested by many on the basis of the missiles' inaccuracy. The CSS-2 has a circular error probable – relating to the radius of a circle into which half of the missiles are likely to land – of about 1–2 km, which would make them less accurate and cost-effective than aircraft-delivered munitions.[146] Meanwhile, Richard Russell suggests that the 'CSS-2 programme could serve as a basis for developing more robust ballistic-missile capabilities. It allows the Saudis to train and nurture a cadre of military personnel expert in ballistic-missile operations'.[147] Moreover, the CSS-2 may not even be kept 'truly operational', and Saudi Arabia has never conducted 'a meaningful operational test'.[148] This further suggests that the CSS-2 is intended less as an instrument of conventional warfighting, and more as a reserve strategic capability.

Finally, Saudi Arabian officials have repeatedly made public and private statements suggesting that they would strongly consider a nuclear response to Iranian weaponisation. In 2011, for instance, former Saudi intelligence chief, Prince Turki Al-Faisal, said in reference to the prospect of Iranian weapons that 'it is our duty toward our nation and people to

---

[143] See 'If the Bombs Go: European Perspectives on NATO's Nuclear Debate', RUSI Whitehall Report 1-11, May 2011.

[144] Bruno Tertrais, 'Kahn's [sic] Nuclear Exports: Was There a State Strategy?', in Henry D Sokolski (ed.), *Pakistan's Nuclear Future: Worries Beyond War* (Carlisle, PA: Strategic Studies Institute, 2008), p. 41.

[145] *NTI.org*, 'Saudi Arabia Missile Profile', November 2011; for more detail on the deal with China, see Yitzhak Shichor, *East Wind over Arabia: Origins and Implications of the Sino-Saudi Missiled Deal*, China Research Monograph No. 35 (Berkeley, CA: Center for Chinese Studies, University of California, 1989).

[146] Russell, 'A Saudi Nuclear Option?', p. 74.

[147] *Ibid.*, p. 73.

[148] Cordesman, *Western Strategic Interests in Saudi Arabia*, p. 257.

consider all possible options, including the possession of these [nuclear] weapons'.[149] Likewise, in 2009, King Abdullah reportedly told former US Middle East envoy Dennis Ross, 'If they [Iran] get nuclear weapons, we will get nuclear weapons'.[150] Earlier that year, Prince Turki had asked a group of foreign diplomats in Riyadh, 'what should the Kingdom do if Iran acquires such [nuclear] weapons ... Invite others to station nuclear weapons in Saudi Arabia?'[151] As a final example, in 2007, a highly classified cable from the US embassy in Riyadh noted that 'Saudi leaders ... have made it clear that the Kingdom would be vulnerable to a nuclear-armed Iran if the Saudis did not also possess a nuclear capability', and that their policy is partly intended 'to buy them time to develop an independent Saudi nuclear deterrent'.[152]

Decoding Saudi Arabian Nuclear Hints

Such signals are important. They far exceed in frequency and intensity those sent by other would-be proliferators, and may indeed reflect a determination to respond in kind to Iranian weaponisation. However, holding in view the five aforementioned factors shaping proliferation choices, these signals must be put in context. So, too, should the potential set of Saudi Arabian nuclear capabilities outlined above.

First, Saudi signals of nuclear intent are just that: signals – or specifically, efforts to shape Iranian and Western perceptions of Saudi policy, so as to deter Iranian weaponisation and encourage Western pressure on Iran to that end. In this sense, they might be seen as equivalent to Israeli threats to attack Iran, intended just as much for Western (and, specifically, American) audiences as Iranian ones. Saudi Arabia has every incentive to make such declarations, but these are costless, non-binding promises; they do not tie Saudi hands (even if they generate limited reputational costs in the event that Riyadh does not follow through on its threats).[153] Indeed, during a February 2012 parliamentary debate in the

---

[149] *New York Times*, 'Prince Hints Saudi Arabia May Join Nuclear Arms Race', 6 December 2011.
[150] Chemi Shalev, 'Dennis Ross: Saudi King Vowed to Obtain Nuclear Bomb after Iran', *Haaretz*, 30 May 2012.
[151] US embassy in Riyadh, 'US Cable: Saudi Views on Iran', 10 January 2009, <http://cables.mrkva.eu/cable.php?id = 186553>, accessed 26 October 2012.
[152] US embassy in Riyadh, 'US Cable: Scenesetter for APHSCT Townsend Visit to Saudi Arabia, 5–8 February 2007', 1 February 2007, <http://cables.mrkva.eu/cable.php?id = 9486>, accessed 26 October 2012.
[153] As Steven Cook notes, 'What is amazing is how many people take the Saudis seriously'; see Steven A Cook, 'Don't Fear a Nuclear Arms Race in the Middle East', *Foreign Policy*, 2 April 2012.

House of Commons, former British Foreign Secretary Jack Straw made precisely this point:[154]

> I hope that we hear less of the suggestion that were Iran to get a nuclear weapons capability, there would automatically be an arms race in the Middle East. I do not believe that. A senior Saudi diplomat said to me, 'I know what we're saying publicly, but do you really think that having told people that there is no need for us to make any direct response to Israel holding nuclear weapons, we could seriously make a case for developing a nuclear weapons capability to deal with another Muslim country?'

Saudi Arabian Views of the US Nuclear Umbrella
Second, if the opaque trickle of information over Saudi Arabian intentions is to be taken seriously, then it should also be noted that Riyadh clearly sees security guarantees as a viable alternative. According to the former US ambassador to Riyadh, Charles Freeman, in 2003, then-King Fahd requested a US nuclear guarantee.[155] In the same year, according to the *Guardian*, 'a strategy paper being considered at the highest levels in Riyadh' set out three options: first, 'To acquire a nuclear capability as a deterrent'; second, 'To maintain or enter into an alliance with an existing nuclear power that would offer protection'; and third, 'To try to reach a regional agreement on having a nuclear-free Middle East'.[156]

The second of these options may allude either to an agreement with Pakistan (or China) or with the United States. However, as arms-control expert Josh Pollack observes, 'the US-Saudi relationship is one of America's most important, enduring, and complex bilateral connections in the Middle East'.[157] Washington and Riyadh are bound by an extremely dense set of strategic, military and economic connections.[158]

To be sure, some of those connections have been under strain, particularly in recent years. The Kingdom was angered and worried by what it perceived as American acquiescence in the overthrow of Hosni Mubarak in 2011. According to one American official, 'they've taken it personally because they question what we'd do if they are next'.[159] Despite

---

[154] Jack Straw, 'Backbench Debate on Iran', *Hansard*, HC Debates, 20 February 2012, Vol. 540, Col. 650.
[155] Tertrais, 'Kahn's [*sic*] Nuclear Exports:', pp. 27–28.
[156] Ewen MacAskill and Ian Traynor, 'Saudis Consider Nuclear Bomb', *Guardian*, 18 September 2003.
[157] Josh Pollack, 'Saudi Arabia and the United States, 1931–2002', *Middle Eastern Review of International Affairs* (Vol. 6, No. 3, September 2002).
[158] James Thomson, 'US Interests and the Fate of the Alliance', *Survival* (Vol. 45, No. 4, 2003).
[159] David E Sanger and Eric Schmitt, 'U.S.-Saudi Tensions Intensify With Mideast Turmoil', *New York Times*, 14 March 2011.

their co-operation, then, Riyadh and Washington, remain divided on questions of the threat posed by Iran, the proper response to it, and the balance between repression and political reform.[160]

In response to regional upheaval, Saudi Arabia has worked to diversify its alliance portfolio. This has included strengthening the security aspects of the GCC, as well as expanding the grouping to take in (non-Gulf) Morocco and Jordan.[161] However, the GCC remains an ineffectual security provider. The 'lack of cooperation, interoperability, and serious exercise activity cripples their ability to act with any unity and makes them more of a facade than a force. It also makes them far more dependent on the US'.[162] Although Riyadh can deepen its relationship with Russia and China over the longer term, neither of these states is in a position to provide the same degree of conventional military and political backing as the United States.

It is important to remember that episodes of Saudi mistrust of the US commitment have occurred before, and the relationship has survived. In 1979, for instance, after the fall of the Shah of Iran, the Carter administration delivered F-15 fighter aircraft to Saudi Arabia, but undercut this gesture by a presidential statement that the aircraft were not armed.[163] It is reasonable to assume therefore that, just as it did three decades ago, the US is likely to remain the most important security provider to Saudi Arabia, and that is likely to provide Saudi Arabia with a viable alternative to seeking its own nuclear means.

A Nuclear Saudi Arabia and Gulf Fears

The third reason that Saudi Arabia's signals of nuclear intent might not be entirely credible is that Riyadh faces a dilemma between nuclear self-help and collective security. This is in at least two senses.

In the first place, a nuclear Saudi Arabia would concern those Gulf States that see a stronger Saudi Arabia as reducing their own autonomy.[164] For example, the smaller states of the Gulf Cooperation Council,

---

[160] Marc Lynch, 'Arab Uprisings: The Saudi Counter-Revolution', POMEPS Briefing No. 5, 9 August 2011, p. 4.

[161] Marc Lynch, 'The What Cooperation Council?', *Foreign Policy*, 11 March 2011; David Aaron, Frederic Wehrey and Brett Andrew Wallace, *The Future of Gulf Security in a Region of Dramatic Change: Mutual Equities and Enduring Relationships* (Santa Monica, CA: RAND Corporation, 2011), p. viii.

[162] Anthony H Cordesman and Aram Nerguizian, 'The Gulf Military Balance in 2010', Center for Strategic and Internation Studies, 23 April 2010.

[163] Kate Amlin, 'Will Saudi Arabia Acquire Nuclear Weapons?', Nuclear Threat Initiative, 1 August 2008.

[164] James Dobbins, Alireza Nader, Dalia Dassa Kaye and Frederic Wehrey, *Coping with a Nuclearizing Iran* (Santa Monica, CA: RAND Corporation, 2011), p. 31.

particularly Oman and Qatar, have more balanced policies towards Iran. Qatar has attempted to normalise Arab relations with Iran, even inviting Iran to the GCC summit in 2007.[165] These states are worried about Saudi Arabia's potential 'hegemonic overreaction' to a nuclear Iran and the possibility that Riyadh might 'exploit the threat from Tehran to win Washington's recognition of Saudi pre-eminence in the Sunni Arab world'.[166] Certainly, fears over Saudi predominance should not be underestimated: the UAE has withdrawn from a Gulf monetary union in opposition to its basing in Riyadh, and in March 2010 there occurred unprecedented naval clashes between Saudi and Emirati vessels over maritime disputes.[167]

Whether or not these threat perceptions would remain unchanged in the aftermath of Iranian weaponisation, and whether this would prompt a balancing against Iran or a 'bandwagoning' with it,[168] depends on a number of factors, such as Iran's behaviour and the availability of security guarantees from other powers, like the United States. The Gulf States may opt for the 'offshore balancer', the United States, rather than the overbearing Saudi Arabia in such a scenario, leaving Saudi Arabia diplomatically isolated. Kristian Coates Ulrichsen of the LSE argues that 'decisions taken since 1991 have integrated each of the GCC states into the American security umbrella on a bilateral basis, and undercut any residual collective approach to security'.[169] This development further structures the Gulf States' incentives in ways that favour the United States. It may therefore be preferable for Saudi Arabia to shun nuclear weapons, limit the fears of its neighbours, and instead lead a regional coalition backed by an American nuclear guarantee.

US Leverage over Saudi Arabia
The second Saudi dilemma flows from the fact that the US is the major supplier of weaponry to the Kingdom. Between 2005 and 2009, 40 per cent of Saudi Arabia's arms imports were of American provenance (a further 42 per cent came from Britain, which, in the Middle East, is likely to follow the contours of US policy).[170] In December 2011, the US finalised a deal to

[165] David Roberts, 'Examining Qatari-Saudi Relations', The Gulf blog, 28 February 2012.
[166] Dassa Kaye and Wehrey, 'A Nuclear Iran', p. 112.
[167] Kristian Coates Ulrichsen, *Insecure Gulf: The End of Certainty and the Transition to the Post-Oil Era* (New York: Columbia University Press, 2001), p. 91.
[168] For explanations of the terms balancing and bandwagoning, see Thomas J Christensen and Jack Snyder, 'Chain Gangs and Passed Bucks: Predicting Alliance Patterns in Multipolarity', *International Organization* (Vol. 44, No. 2, Spring 1990).
[169] Ulrichsen, *Insecure Gulf*, p. 92.
[170] Carina Solmirano and Pieter D Wezeman, 'Military Spending and Arms Procurement in the Gulf States', SIPRI Fact Sheet October 2010, p. 3.

sell advanced military equipment worth $30 billion to Saudi Arabia.[171] Between 1990 and 2011, US arms sales in constant prices to Saudi Arabia totalled $14.7 billion, far higher than the $4.6 billion paid to the second-highest supplier in that period, the UK.[172] Arms sales do not automatically produce commensurate political leverage, but they are reflective of Saudi Arabia's dependence on the US for its long-term, qualitative military strength.

Moreover, there is evidence that the US can, and does, successfully pressure Saudi Arabia. Richard Russell notes that 'at least one scholar has suggested that Saudi Arabia was considering the establishment of a weapons-related nuclear infrastructure, but that strong American diplomatic intervention convinced Riyadh to abandon the idea'.[173]

Another, better evidenced, example dates to 1988: when the US learnt of the earlier transfer of CSS-2 missiles to Saudi Arabia, it once more used its leverage to compel Saudi Arabia to sign the NPT as a compensatory measure. After mounting concern in Congress, congressional majorities passed resolutions against the sale of ground-support equipment for Airborne Warning and Control System aircraft that had been supplied to Saudi Arabia in 1981. The administration also suspended sale of military equipment worth another $450 million.[174]

Admittedly, Saudi Arabia is insulated in at least one important respect. Its status as OPEC's largest oil producer and the world's second-largest oil exporter means that Saudi Arabia wields substantial influence over world oil prices, and therefore over global economic conditions. In the aftermath of Iranian weaponisation, Iran would likely be subject to even more punitive energy-related sanctions than those in force now. It would not therefore be a realistic option to similarly coerce Saudi Arabia without thereby causing politically unacceptable rises in oil prices.

However, this does not mean that Saudi Arabia could not be punished in other ways. Saudi Arabian private and official investments in the United States amount to hundreds of billions of dollars, and US personnel provide vital training for Saudi Arabian forces.[175] Nevertheless, although Riyadh is not without friends in Congress, congressional concern would be directed at the security of Israel. Saudi Arabia does not have diplomatic relations with Israel, maintaining an economic boycott against

---

[171] Mark Landler and Stephen Lee Myers, 'With $30 Billion Arms Deal, U.S. Bolsters Saudi Ties', *New York Times*, 29 December 2011.
[172] 'Table of Arms Exports to Saudi Arabia, 1990–2011', SIPRI, October 2012. Figures are expressed in 1990 dollars.
[173] The original claim is that of Yair Evron, on the basis of 'private information', cited in Russell, 'A Saudi Nuclear Option?', p. 78. No date is supplied.
[174] Lippman, 'Nuclear Weapons and Saudi Strategy', p. 4; see also Shichor, *East Wind over Arabia*, p. 60.
[175] Lippman, *ibid.*, p. 6.

the country. The nuclearisation of both Iran and Saudi Arabia would provoke alarm and fear amongst Israel's proponents in the US. Even as the White House would likely recognise the particular importance of maintaining ties with Saudi Arabia in the aftermath of Iranian weaponisation, it would face difficulties in resisting this domestic political pressure. Riyadh would surely be wary of jeopardising ties with its pre-eminent patron and ally at the very moment that the Kingdom would be seen as being at its most vulnerable.

It should also be remembered that, although Saudi Arabia is largely insulated from economic pressure – and would be even more so in the event of a proliferation chain in the Middle East since oil prices would shoot upwards and increase oil revenue – its would-be nuclear supplier, Pakistan, is not. Even with Saudi economic assistance, Pakistan would be wary of facing further international opprobrium, given its chequered proliferation history. As one former official of the Strategic Plans Division, Pakistan's nuclear steward, puts it, the deployment of Pakistani warheads on Saudi Arabian soil would be 'worse than the Cuban missile crisis', with all that implies for Pakistan's own security.[176]

Much would depend on the state of US-Pakistani relations. Were they to have irredeemably deteriorated, Pakistan might not consider American opprobrium and political pressure to be a particularly great deterrent. Pakistan's civil-military balance might also be significant, with the military perhaps more incentivised to break international norms and extend assistance to Riyadh, and civilians possibly more desirous of maintaining good diplomatic relations with the international community.[177] A final factor may be the importance of personal relationships. As the Emirati commentator Sultan Al-Qassemi notes, 'the solid Saudi relationship with Pakistan is heavily dependent on close co-ordination between the interior and intelligence authorities of both states in which [Prince] Nayef played a significant role'.[178] Nayef died in June 2012; if there is a lack of institutional continuity, Pakistan may question the Saudi commitment to shielding Pakistan from the consequences of proliferation.

These reasons, taken together, suggest that Saudi Arabia has strong disincentives to proliferate, and that these should be considered alongside the pressures that would undoubtedly result from Iranian weaponisation.

---

[176] Bruno Tertrais, 'Pakistan's Nuclear and WMD Programmes: Status, Evolution and Risks', Non-Proliferation Papers No. 19, EU Non-Proliferation Consortium, July 2012, p. 16.

[177] That said, A Q Khan has claimed that Pakistan's civilian leaders, including then-Prime Minister Benazir Bhutto, approved his nuclear transfers to other states. See Rob Crilly, 'AQ Khan Claims Benazir Bhutto Ordered Nuclear Sale', *Daily Telegraph*, 17 September 2012.

[178] Sultan Souud Al-Qassemi, 'Prince Nayef's Death Makes a Big Difference in the Middle East', *Guardian*, 19 July 2012.

Sceptics, like Edelman and Montgomery, argue that 'the United States was able to deter a nuclear-armed Soviet Union during the Cold War, but the foundations of its security arrangements then – formal treaty guarantees and large U.S. military deployments on the territory of its allies – are unlikely to materialize again soon'.[179]

This likely underestimates the degree to which the US is deeply concerned over second-order proliferation and potential Gulf appeasement of Iran, both outcomes that it fears will result from a nuclear Iran in the event of US inaction. Moreover, the US already has a history of deployments on Gulf territory, even if these have proven politically problematic in the past. Some argue that in order for nuclear guarantees to be credible, the US must station nuclear weapons on Gulf soil. This would be politically controversial and, in generating a new major role for US nuclear weapons, would undercut many of the efforts in recent years to downgrade the role of such weapons in US defence posture.[180]

However, this may not even be a necessary step. US nuclear weapons have not been located in South Korea for over two decades, and were never publicly stationed in Japan; yet the US (successfully) provided extended deterrence assurance to both of these allies.[181]

Egypt

Egypt presents a more ambiguous case than Saudi Arabia. Egyptian-Iranian ties were severed in 1980 following the Iranian revolution, Egypt's granting of sanctuary to the deposed Shah, and Iranian opposition to Egypt's peace with Israel in the 1970s. Egyptian foreign policy under President Hosni Mubarak saw an alignment with the Saudi-led anti-Iranian bloc, which was connected both to the Mubarak regime's pro-US orientation, and to its concern over Iran's support of 'rejectionist' Palestinian groups in competition with Egypt-backed 'moderates'.[182] Mubarak once told George Mitchell, then-US envoy to the Middle East, that Iranians were 'liars' and that negotiations should take place only on the understanding that 'you don't believe a word they say'.[183] In 2009, the US embassy in Cairo observed that 'Mubarak has a visceral hatred for the Islamic

---

[179] Edelman, Krepinevich, Jr and Montgomery, 'The Dangers of a Nuclear Iran'.

[180] *New York Times*, 'The Nuclear "Implementation Study"', 11 March 2012; Trevor Taylor, 'Implications of the US Nuclear Posture Review', *RUSI.org*, 8 April 2010.

[181] Japanese ports were used, however. See Martin Fackler, 'Japan Says It Allowed U.S. Nuclear Ships to Port', *New York Times*, 9 March 2010.

[182] Richard Spencer, 'Egypt and Iran Forging Closer Links with Ambassadors Plan', *Daily Telegraph*, 19 April 2011.

[183] Leaked US cable cited in Seyed Hossein Mousavian, *The Iranian Nuclear Crisis: A Memoir* (Washington, DC: Carnegie Endowment for International Peace, 2012), p. 6.

Republic...denouncing [Iran] for seeking to destabilize Egypt and the region', and judged that 'there is no doubt that Egypt sees Iran as its greatest long-term threat'.[184]

However, following the Egyptian revolution of 2011, Iran appointed its first ambassador to Cairo in three decades.[185] In February 2012, Egypt allowed two Iranian naval vessels to pass through the Suez Canal en route to Syria for the first time since ties were severed.[186] Egypt's geographical distance from Iran also limits the scale of the threat perceived.

Egypt's evolving democratic institutions may further mitigate Egyptian-Iranian tensions. Egypt's parliament, elected in early 2012, is dominated by Islamists, most belonging to the Muslim Brotherhood's political party but a significant minority to more extreme Salafist groupings. That parliament, though currently dissolved, might be expected to further dilute Mubarak-era anti-Iran policies if it grows in political stature. Muslim Brotherhood members hold a diverse range of views on Iran. Mehdi Khalaji, a former Iranian theologian, suggests that 'the Muslim Brotherhood is Iran's main potential political ally in a new Egypt' and that 'Iran is pushing for the empowerment of the Muslim Brotherhood'.[187] In June 2012, the Egyptian presidency was won by Mohammed Morsi, the candidate of the Muslim Brotherhood, who subsequently visited Tehran in August 2012 for the Non-Aligned Movement summit and broke with Western policy to reach out to Iran on the issue of the conflict in Syria.

It is too early to judge whether the shift in Egypt's stance is durable. Both the political structure of the post-revolutionary Egyptian state, and the foreign-policy apparatus of the government, remains in flux. If the Egyptian armed forces continue to exercise power over the medium term, and to dominate an enfeebled parliament or presidency, it is possible that policy will retain a status quo bias, with bureaucrats and military officers hewing to an anti-Iran line, and liaising with like-minded counterparts in Saudi Arabia and other anti-Iran states.

It is also possible that political disorder in Egypt will increase further. Under such conditions, Egypt might be rendered diplomatically ineffectual, and play little role in the regional balance of power, or in events outside of its immediate neighbourhood. Given the lengthy timeline in which Iran could realistically develop nuclear weapons, it is impossible to forecast Egypt's strategic orientation with any accuracy.

---

[184] US embassy in Cairo, 'US Cable: Scenesetter for Requested Egyptian FM Aboul Gheit Meeting with the Secretary', 9 February 2009.

[185] *Haaretz*, 'Report: Iran Appoints First Ambassador to Egypt in 30 Years', 19 April 2011.

[186] *Al-Ahram*, 'Israel Eyes Suez Trip of Iran Warships with Worry', 21 February 2011.

[187] Mehdi Khalaji, 'Iran on Egypt's Muslim Brotherhood', The Iran Primer blog, United States Institute of Peace, 25 February 2011.

However, whoever leads Egypt over the coming years will not necessarily see Iranian nuclear weapons as a major threat deserving of a similarly major response. As Steven Cook observes, 'Pakistan's perception of the threat posed by India – a state with which it has fought four wars since 1947 – is far more acute than how either Egypt or Turkey perceive the Iranian challenge'.[188]

There is a clear precedent for this in Egyptian history: its non-response to the Israeli acquisition of nuclear weapons in the late 1960s, at a time when Israel was the major preoccupation of the Egyptian armed forces. Egypt would therefore suffer no greater reputational cost in failing to respond in kind to Iranian weaponisation than it did with respect to Israel.

Egypt did develop a nuclear infrastructure in the 1950s, and – until its peace with Israel – did not allow IAEA inspections at its Inshas nuclear research centre. However, neither Sadat nor Mubarak made an effort to develop nuclear weapons technology.[189] Although there were persistent reports of clandestine nuclear ties between Egypt and Colonel Qadhafi's Libya, said to date to the 1970s and including both nuclear and missile technology, these will anyway have been disrupted by the change of regime in Libya in 2011. In May 2009, an Egyptian diplomat privately told US counterparts that Egypt had been offered nuclear weapons and associated technology by Soviet scientists in the aftermath of the Soviet Union's break-up, but that it had rejected such overtures.[190]

Egypt possesses neither an indigenous enrichment programme nor a nuclear power reactor, and other aspects of its civilian nuclear programme have progressed slowly and with difficulty.[191] An upgraded nuclear programme is also likely to be prohibitively expensive. Ongoing political instability, with the attendant strain on Egypt's finances and managerial coherence, is likely to hinder any such effort. Robert Einhorn, the US State Department's special adviser for non-proliferation and arms control, has argued that Egypt is unlikely to be able to procure the necessary equipment and technology detection and, that if it managed to do so, it would be four to six years before it was able to produce fissile material.[192]

---

[188] Cook, 'Don't Fear a Nuclear Arms Race in the Middle East'.

[189] *Ibid.*

[190] Julian Borger, 'Wikileaks Cables: Egypt "Turned Down" Black-Market Nuclear Weapons Deal', *Guardian*, 19 December 2010.

[191] Bowen and Kidd, 'The Nuclear Capabilities and Ambitions of Iran's Neighbors', pp. 61–62.

[192] Robert J Einhorn, 'Egypt: Frustrated but Still on a Non-Nuclear Course', in Kurt M Campbell, Robert J Einhorn and Mitchell B Reiss (eds), *The Nuclear Tipping Point: Why States Reconsider Their Nuclear Choices* (Washington, DC: Brookings Institution, 2004), p. 57.

Egypt's newer research reactor would be able to produce around 6.6 kg of plutonium per year – just under 1.5 kg short of the amount necessary for one bomb, according to the IAEA (but in excess of more conservative thresholds); but this reactor is under IAEA safeguards, meaning that any diversion of nuclear material would be detected.[193] Egypt does possess a range of ballistic missiles and fighter jets that could serve as potential delivery systems, but these would each have to be modified to carry nuclear payloads – again, at a steep cost.[194]

Egypt also faces a set of potential diplomatic costs to weaponisation similar to those faced by Saudi Arabia – notably, the potential loss of American financial and military aid, and US congressional hostility to the weaponisation of a historic Israeli adversary – without any of the same economic insulation, such as oil revenue, to cushion any decision to acquire weapons.

Moreover, Egypt is even *more* dependent on US assistance than Saudi Arabia. During 2006–10, 60 per cent of Egypt's imports of major arms came from the US, including M1A1 tanks and M113 armoured vehicles (recall that Saudi Arabia received only 40 per cent of its arms from the US between 2005 and 2009).[195] Although the political marginalisation of Egypt's armed forces might change this source of US leverage – indeed, a future civilian-dominated government might welcome the opportunity to see US assistance to the army shrink – this is by no means inevitable. The military might prefer nuclear weapons to conventional weapons, but this is typically not the choice of military organisations that have faced such decisions in the past.[196]

This assessment of Egyptian behaviour is clearly sensitive to the trajectory of Egypt's political transition, while Israel's response to any Iranian weaponisation – and particularly an overt Israeli test or a declaration of Israeli nuclear status – could also be an important factor. However, any Egyptian effort to develop nuclear weapons would be difficult, lengthy and costly.

---

[193] Bowen and Kidd, 'The Nuclear Capabilities and Ambitions of Iran's Neighbors', p. 64.

[194] Richard L Russell, *Weapons Proliferation and War in the Greater Middle East: Strategic Contest* (Abingdon: Routledge, 2005), p. 64; Cordesman and Al-Rodhan, *Gulf Military Forces in an Era of Asymmetric Wars*, pp. 169–74.

[195] Paul Holtom et al., 'Trends in International Arms Transfers, 2010', SIPRI Fact Sheet, March 2011, p. 7.

[196] For instance, see Perkovich, *India's Nuclear Bomb*, p. 152.

Turkey

Turkey's relationship with Iran is similarly complex, and includes various elements of competition,[197] the two states having vied for influence in both Iraq and Palestine. With regards to the latter, Turkey's ruling AK Party has effectively abandoned Turkey's alliance with Israel and thereby won regional popular approval.

They have also found themselves on opposite sides of the battle over Syria (with Iran supporting the Assad regime, and Turkey sheltering, arming and assisting parts of the political and armed opposition). Furthermore, they have clashed over Turkey's participation in hosting the radar for NATO's missile-defence system, fuelling belligerent rhetoric from them both over this issue. Iran's nuclear and missile programme was featured as the primary threat in Turkey's 2005 Red Book, formally called the National Security Policy Document.[198]

These irritants have manifested themselves in different ways. Turkey complains that in 2004–05, the IRGC forced a Turkish-led consortium to withdraw its involvement in operating Tehran's new airport. Iran also annulled a mobile phone tender that had been won by a Turkish company, and cut gas supplies to Turkey in 2007 and 2008 to prioritise domestic demand.[199]

At the same time, the Turkish government's aspirations for regional leadership have driven extensive engagement with its neighbours, including Iran. The phrase 'zero problems' has sometimes been used as shorthand for this multidirectional activism, intended to repair frayed relations and deepen economic integration.[200] To this end, Turkey's foreign minister has made over sixty visits to Syria since 2009.[201]

Furthermore, in 2010, Turkey voted against the imposition of further sanctions on Iran at the UN. That same year, Turkey worked with Brazil to offer Iran an alternative fuel-swap agreement, which met with frustration from US officials who were attempting to shore up those sanctions already in place. More broadly in relation to Iran's nuclear programme, Turkey's ruling AK Party has been 'highly sceptical about sanctions and rules out any military action', and 'argue[s] that trade ties and travel can ease Iran's

---

[197] Philipp C Bleek and Aaron Stein, 'Turkey and America Face Iran', *Survival* (Vol. 54, No. 2, April–May 2012), pp. 27–28.

[198] Dobbins, Nader, Kaye and Wehrey, *Coping with a Nuclearizing Iran.*

[199] International Crisis Group, 'In Heavy Waters: Iran's Nuclear Program, the Risk of War and Lessons from Turkey', Middle East and Europe Report No. 116, 23 February 2012, p. 21.

[200] Morton Abramowitz and Henri J Barkey, 'Turkey's Transformers: The AKP Sees Big', *Foreign Affairs* (Vol. 88, No. 6, November/December 2009), p. 118; for the Turkish foreign minister's own exposition of the term, see Ahmet Davutoglu, 'Turkey's Zero-Problems Foreign Policy', *Foreign Policy*, 20 May 2010.

[201] *Economist*, 'Turkey and Syria: One Problem with a Neighbour', 20 August 2011.

friction with the West'. However, this position may not reflect affinity with Iran so much as concern over the impact of sanctions on Turkish commercial interests in the country:[202] indeed, Turkish exports to Iran, which had grown twelve-fold in the past decade to over $3.5 billion in 2011, fell by a quarter in the two-month period between December 2011 and January 2012. All Turkish banks except one have ceased processing payments for Iranian customers, and the number of Turkish tourists to Iran has plunged.[203] All of this has resulted mostly from *bilateral* sanctions – that is, those outside the purview of the UN and beyond the control of either Turkey or the UN Security Council.

It should also be noted that Iran – with its own Kurdish minority – has recently co-operated with Turkey in the latter's campaign against the Kurdish PKK rebel group, even though Turkey had threatened war against Iran in 1998 over the latter's hosting of a PKK leader. In late 2011, Iran and Turkey also announced that they would jointly pursue an Iraq-based group, the PJAK, which Iran had shelled the previous year.[204]

Even where Turkey explicitly adopts anti-Iran policies, it seeks to do so with caution. When NATO held missile-defence talks during its 2011 Lisbon Summit, Turkey – despite hosting a radar system very obviously designed to detect Iranian missiles – insisted that Iran could not be specified as a named threat to NATO in the alliance's Strategic Concept.[205]

Shifts in any of these factors might correspondingly alter Turkish threat perceptions. This might come about as a result of political changes in Iraq or Palestine, such as a political crisis that sees pro-Iran factions in Baghdad seize greater control outside of constitutional arrangements. It might also stem from a potential military intervention by Turkey in northern Syria; or, perhaps, relations could be strained by a weakening of Iran's co-operation on containing Kurdish groups.

There is little doubt that relations have deteriorated in the two years since 2010. However, Western analyses are prone to overlook the nuance in Turkey's Iran policy, a nuance that has not been washed out by differences over Syria and missile defence. Turkey has consistently held to a more moderate position than the P5 + 1, has typically been less prone to see Iran's nuclear activities in malign terms, and has borne diplomatic costs itself in defending that position. However, that also indicates that Ankara might view Iranian acquisition of nuclear weapons as especially galling,

---

[202] International Crisis Group, 'In Heavy Waters', p. 4.
[203] Joe Parkinson, 'Iran Sanctions Put Wrinkle in Turkish Trade', *Wall Street Journal*, 19 March 2012.
[204] Kenneth Katzman, 'Iran: U.S. Concerns and Policy Responses', Congressional Research Service, 23 March 2012, p. 21.
[205] Rick Gladstone, 'Turkey to Install U.S.-Designed Radar, in a Move Seen as Blunting Iran's Missiles', *New York Times*, 2 September 2011.

and a diplomatic betrayal. Iranian weaponisation may therefore lead Turkey to view Iran as untrustworthy, and that in turn may deeply affect Turkish security perceptions.

Some Turkish officials have indicated that they would seek nuclear weapons in response to Iranian weaponisation. Two former commanders of the Turkish air force, Generals Halis Burhan and Ergin Celasin, have declared that 'if Iran develops nuclear weapons, Turkey should do the same so as to be able to preserve the balance of power between the two countries and also in the region'.[206] Jean-Loup Samaan suggests that, 'although these views are not officially endorsed by Turkey's government, they reflect the state of the national security debate'.[207] Indeed, according to one public opinion poll, 53.9 per cent of those Turks surveyed believe that NATO's security umbrella is not sufficient to counter the threat of a nuclear Iran, and that Turkey should develop its own nuclear weapons; in contrast, only 34.8 per cent disagree.[208]

However, there are a number of reasons why Turkey is unlikely to take this path. First, Turkey is a member of NATO and, as such, already enjoys longstanding nuclear protection. Although Turkish-US ties have been strained over the past decade following incidents like the Turkish parliament's rejection of US deployments on Turkish soil as part of the 2003 Iraq War, these strains have not altered the fundamentals of Turkey's position within the Alliance. Turkey's hosting of the radar element of NATO's missile-defence shield further indicates its perception of NATO as a suitable vehicle for long-term security.

Second, many of the institutional prerequisites for successful extended deterrence already exist. Turkey hosts two US air force bases, one of which – Izmir Air Station – includes the headquarters of NATO's Allied Air Component Command for Southern Europe. In addition, Turkey's 39th Air Base Wing hosts around sixty to seventy B61 gravity bombs at Incirlik air force base near Adana, with ten to twenty of those designated for Turkey and the remainder for the US.[209] The Turkish air force cannot deliver these weapons itself (although this is contested, and thirty Turkish F-16s are due to receive stopgap modification to carry the next generation of US nuclear bombs), as it lacks suitable aircraft. The US does not station appropriate aircraft inside Turkey; however, these are both steps that could be taken in the aftermath of Iranian weaponisation and would be more

[206] Dobbins, Nader, Kaye and Wehrey, *Coping with a Nuclearizing Iran*, p. 51.
[207] Samaan, 'The Day after Iran Goes Nuclear', p. 5.
[208] Center for Economics and Foreign Policy Studies, 'Public Opinion Surveys of Turkish Foreign Policy 2012/1: Conditional Support for Nuclear Armament', <http://www.edam.org.tr/document/Edam2012Survey1.pdf>, accessed 26 October 2012.
[209] Robert S Norris and Hans M Kristensen, 'US Tactical Nuclear Weapons in Europe, 2011', *Bulletin of the Atomic Scientists* (Vol. 67, No. 1, 2010), pp. 66–67.

preferable, from the point of view of both Ankara and others, than a Turkish effort to develop an indigenous nuclear capability.[210]

Turkish faith in these external guarantees cannot be taken for granted. For one thing, the Dutch parliament's decision to halt procurement of the F-35 means that, like Germany, it might have no designated successor for its F-16s, which will go out of service in 2025, and therefore no future nuclear-delivery capability.[211] Furthermore, Turkey might not want to be the only remaining country, apart from Italy, which hosts NATO nuclear weapons if Germany and the Netherlands no longer do so.[212]

The uncertainty over NATO's tactical nuclear weapons reflects a broader and deeper uncertainty over the dependability of the Alliance as a whole. Turkey's 1952 accession to the Alliance was contested, and Turkey has routinely worried about whether it could rely on its allies in the context of a Middle Eastern, rather than European, threat.[213] These anxieties grew after the US imposed an arms embargo on Turkey in 1974 in response to the latter's invasion of Cyprus.[214] However, as Sinan Ulgen writes, 'the only circumstance where [Turkish nuclear weapons] would acquire a degree of likelihood is a breakdown of Turkey's security relationship with the United States'.[215]

Yet the relationship would probably be at its most robust in exactly the circumstances when it would be needed. In the immediate aftermath of any Iranian acquisition of a nuclear weapon, the US would be all the more incentivised to preserve and deepen its security relationship with Turkey – not least because the European missile-defence system, and therefore Turkish co-operation in hosting the radar, would become crucial.

Third, Turkey would struggle to produce nuclear weapons even if it sought to do so. It has 'no fissile material, cannot mine or enrich uranium, and does not possess the technology to reprocess spent fuel, all of which are required for nuclear weapons development'.[216] Wyn Bowen and Joanna Kidd conclude likewise: 'given the openness of Turkey's nuclear research programme, small uranium reserves, and lack of enrichment and

---

[210] Sinan Ulgen, 'Turkey and the Bomb', *carnegieendowment.org*, February 2012, p. 12.

[211] Kingston Reif, 'Dutch Parliament Says No to the F-35', Nukes of Hazard blog, 9 July 2012.

[212] George Perkovich, Malcolm Chalmers, Steven Pifer, Paul Schulte and Jaclyn Tandler, 'Looking beyond the Chicago Summit: Nuclear Weapons in Europe and the Future of NATO', *carnegieendowment.org*, April 2012, pp. 4–5.

[213] Ian O Lesser, 'Turkey, Iran and Nuclear Risks', in Sokolski and Clawson (eds), *Getting Ready for a Nuclear-Ready Iran*, p. 90.

[214] Fotios Moustakis, *The Greek–Turkish Relationship and NATO* (London: Frank Cass, 2003), p. 41.

[215] Ulgen, 'Turkey and the Bomb', p. 1.

[216] Cook, 'Don't Fear a Nuclear Arms Race in the Middle East'.

reprocessing capabilities, it is difficult to believe that Ankara would develop a nuclear weapons programme in the near future'.[217] The absence of any enrichment capabilities, and the difficulty of obtaining these in the aftermath of Iranian weaponisation (when any potential suppliers would be well aware of Turkey's heightened interest in producing fissile material), is the greatest obstacle to Turkish nuclear weapons.[218]

These three reasons ought to temper proliferation alarmism about Turkey, but they should also alert policy-makers to the importance of alliance dynamics in averting second-order proliferation.

Other States

A nuclear Iran would also have important implications for states other than those discussed above.

Israel is the nuclear-armed state perhaps most directly affected by, and most concerned about, Iranian weaponisation. Setting aside the question of a preventive Israeli military strike on Iran, which is explored later, it is important to consider how Israel would respond in the aftermath of an Iranian acquisition of nuclear weapons.

It is likely that Israel would at least consider altering its policy of opacity, either by declaring its nuclear status or issuing strong signals just short of such a declaration. Although Iran is perfectly aware of the existence of Israeli nuclear weapons, and a declaration would not change this, the attenuation of opacity might be seen as a simple way of increasing the credibility of Israel's deterrent capability.

However, this is not inevitable. Israel's decision in this regard would, of course, be affected by Iran's own choice – the more limited and opaque the process of Iranian weaponisation, the greater the likelihood that Israeli policy would hew to the status quo. Israel would also face similar incentives as Iran to avoid giving any other states reason to proliferate further, and might therefore prefer to issue private signals to Iran rather than public ones, perhaps delivered through intermediaries. One Israeli study argues that 'the establishment of direct communications between Israel and Iran could serve as an important mechanism in redressing dangers involved in Iranian weaponisation'.[219]

---

[217] Bowen and Kidd, 'The Nuclear Capabilities and Ambitions of Iran's Neighbors', p. 66.

[218] Ulgen, 'Turkey and the Bomb', pp. 15–21.

[219] Yair Evron, 'An Israel-Iran Balance of Nuclear Deterrence: Seeds of Instability', in Ephraim Kam (ed.), *Israel and a Nuclear Iran: Implications for Arms Control, Deterrence, and Defense*, Memorandum No. 94 (Tel Aviv: Institute for National Security Studies, 2008), p. 60.

Israel would almost certainly accelerate its missile-defence efforts, although these have been advancing very rapidly in any case.[220] Given that Israel is most concerned about Iranian asymmetric warfare prosecuted from behind a nuclear shield, it would also make sense for Israel to focus efforts on improving the *conventional* capabilities necessary for limited wars under the nuclear threshold. That might require clearer Israeli signalling to shape Iranian expectations – for example, a clear signal that Israel would forcibly interdict weapons shipments to Lebanon regardless of their origin and handlers.

The implications of a nuclear Iran also extend beyond the Middle East. India, which has stated its opposition to a nuclear Iran, would be concerned about any Pakistani proliferation to Saudi Arabia. Any Pakistani nuclear forces on Saudi Arabian soil – whether under Pakistani, Saudi or joint command – could complicate India's targeting policies and numerical requirements. Ever since a doctrinal shift in 2003, Indian officials have signalled that 'credible' minimum deterrence 'must take into account the arsenal size and posture of both of India's nuclear neighbours', and that India's nuclear requirements are flexible.[221] If Pakistani assistance to Saudi Arabia puts upwards pressure on Pakistan's already rapid fissile-material production, India may be unable to distinguish what proportion of this is destined for Saudi Arabia. Such 'excess' production is inherently dual-use, and might therefore prompt India to adopt worst-case estimates of the Pakistani arsenal size, with implications for India's own posture.

Over the longer term, India may also come to see the Iranian nuclear arsenal as a security concern. India currently imports 75 per cent of its total oil requirements, of which 80 per cent comes from the Gulf, a region that also hosts 4 million Indian migrant workers. India also has a defence co-operation relationship with Qatar and Oman, and a 'strategic partnership' with Saudi Arabia.[222] As the US focus shifts to Asia, and Indian naval capabilities grow, India may assume greater security responsibilities in the Gulf, bringing it into more direct contact with Iran.

The Indo-Iranian relationship itself is under strain: for example, in June 2012, Indian investigators found Iranian involvement in an attempted assassination of an Israeli diplomat in Delhi.[223] If India comes to see Iran as a state of greater concern, it may in due course be forced to consider Iranian nuclear capabilities when it assesses its own nuclear requirements – even if such a shift only occurred over decades.

---

[220] Uzi Rubin, 'Missile Defense and Israel's Deterrence against a Nuclear Iran', in Kam (ed.), *Israel and a Nuclear Iran*.
[221] Sagan, 'The Evolution of Pakistani and Indian Nuclear Doctrine', p. 247.
[222] Ulrichsen, *Insecure Gulf*, p. 82.
[223] Jason Burke, 'Iran was Behind Bomb Plot against Israeli Diplomats, Investigators Find', *Guardian*, 17 June 2012.

Pakistan, meanwhile, would face a different set of challenges. Its relationship with Iran is afflicted by a number of irritants, most of them focused on the common border. The present Pakistani government has improved ties with Tehran, but it is uncertain whether these improvements will outlive the precariously balanced civilian incumbents. President Asif Ali Zardari has made particular efforts to engage with Tehran, but this is perceived to have come at a cost to Islamabad's relationship with Riyadh.[224] Moreover, the relationship suffered a setback in October 2009 after a Pakistan-based militant group, Jundullah, was blamed for a major attack on IRGC commanders in southeastern Iran. President Ahmadinejad himself publicly blamed 'certain officials in Pakistan'.[225]

Pakistan's military, which is the real arbiter of Pakistan's nuclear posture and policy, will most likely determine for itself the implications of a nuclear Iran without recourse to civilian opinion. The military's historic record of inflating threats does not bode well, and Iranian-Pakistani friction is especially likely to grow as the two states line up on different sides of a post-ISAF and post-American Afghanistan. However, while any such threat perceptions are likely to be limited in scale, they could serve to justify a further expansion in Pakistan's nuclear ambitions.

Pakistan would also face a difficult choice if Saudi Arabia requested nuclear assistance. Any refusal would jeopardise a key financial and diplomatic relationship, but acceptance could induce severe punishment from the United States and the international community.

A number of other states not discussed here – including Russia, China, France, Britain and emerging powers with an interest in nuclear technology, like Brazil – would all be impacted in various ways by a nuclear Iran, as would the non-proliferation regime as a whole.

---

[224] *Guardian*, 'State Department Cables: Saudis Distrust Pakistan's Shia President Zardari', 1 December 2010.
[225] Atul Aneja, 'Iran Puts Ties with Pakistan to Test', *The Hindu*, 19 October 2012.

V. CONCLUSION

The re-election of President Barack Obama marks the most significant four-year period in the Iranian nuclear crisis so far. As sanctions ravage the Iranian economy and the diplomatic process festers, Iran's nuclear enrichment grows rapidly. The IAEA continues to allege that Iran conducted weapons-related research, continued some aspects of that research even after 2003, and refuses to allow the agency the necessary access to conclude otherwise.

Although the threat of an Israeli military strike appears to have receded for now, it has not disappeared. Israeli Prime Minister Benjamin Netanyahu's speech to the UN General Assembly in September 2012 suggests that Israel wishes to draw its red line for military action at the point at which Iran acquires a certain amount of MEU (when the figure of 240 kg was put to Netanyahu, he did not contest it), even before Iran makes any attempt to enrich that to weapons-grade material. Netanyahu placed that point at 'next spring [or] at most next summer'. The United States has not articulated its own red lines, despite intense Israeli pressure to do so, but it would probably want to wait until after any Iranian decision to enrich uranium beyond 20 per cent, which would make Iranian intentions clear.

The re-elected Obama administration is likely to have more freedom of manoeuvre to explore compromises in talks with Iran, but it might take until the summer of 2013 until Iran has a corresponding flexibility. This would mean a tense and volatile eight-month period in which Iran's economy will further deteriorate, its political system will be stressed by the presidential elections, and its stockpiles of enriched uranium and its enrichment capacity might both continue to grow. In short, there is a disjunction between the political timetable and the timetable of the Iranian programme, which makes the period after the spring of 2013 fraught with risks. As explained in Chapter II, the fall of the Assad regime could exacerbate Iranian vulnerabilities and shock the Iranian system into upgrading the importance of the nuclear programme. So, too, could political instability within Iran, particularly if this inhibited the P5 + 1 from engaging in talks with the regime.

However, Israel's military options remain highly limited.[1] As such, it is likely that Israel will have to accept American red lines. Unless Iran itself takes certain steps – such as expelling or restricting IAEA inspectors, breaking IAEA safeguards, or starting the operation of the heavy-water reactor at Arak – the US has every incentive to be patient until Iran's presidential elections conclude and the conditions are more propitious for a deal. Unless Iran actually wishes to accept the risks entailed in a nuclear breakout, something that is exceedingly unlikely in the absence of a major shock, Iran should be pragmatic enough to avoid these steps. This suggests that Iran may resume converting MEU into (non-enrichable) fuel – as it had been doing for months but then, by November 2012, stopped – thereby reducing the amount immediately available for a bomb.

However, there are some steps that Iran might see as relatively innocuous that would alarm the US: for instance, the movement of large stockpiles of LEU into Fordow might be interpreted by the US as a precursor to breakout. For this reason, the US should consider privately signalling at least some of its red lines to Iran, even if this risks encouraging Iran to continue right up to that point.

If and when diplomatic talks resume in earnest, with greater flexibility on each side, a deal should be possible. As outlined in Chapter III, the West's focus should be on stretching out the time it would take Iran to breakout to nuclear weapons, increasing the likelihood that breakout and other illicit nuclear activities would be detected, and securing Iran's co-operation with the IAEA.

The West's primary objectives to this end should be stopping Iran's enrichment of uranium to 20 per cent, and having Iran re-apply the modified Code 3.1 of its Subsidiary Arrangements with the IAEA (obliging Iran to report any decisions to construct new nuclear facilities), as well as ratifying and re-adopting the Additional Protocol to its Safeguards Agreement (giving the IAEA broader powers of verification). Iran should be offered limited and reversible sanctions relief for each of these steps, with the complete lifting of nuclear-related sanctions promised once Iran is given a clean bill of health by the IAEA. If Iran proved unco-operative at any point, these sanctions could be re-imposed. In short, any deal would allow Iran to keep enriching uranium to lower levels, but only under restrictive conditions.

It should also be understood that a deal would probably not lead to the removal of sanctions imposed for non-nuclear reasons, such as Iran's human rights record. It is politically impossible for Western states to remove all such sanctions, but these must be calibrated: if Iran believes that even the resolution of the nuclear dispute would leave

---

[1] Israel's military options were examined in Chapter IV. See also Mark Perry, 'The Entebbe Option', *Foreign Policy*, 27 September 2012.

its predicament unchanged, it would perceive little reason to make concessions. A comprehensive agreement addressing non-nuclear areas of dispute would be needed for complete sanctions relief, but this is far harder to envisage.

If the process of reaching a nuclear deal is not started in 2013, there is a risk that sanctions become entrenched for a much longer period, potentially fracturing the cohesion of the anti-Iran bloc (much as the anti-Saddam bloc fragmented in the late 1990s), as well as weakening and embittering the Iranian regime without dislodging it or forcing it to abandon its nuclear activities.

Over the longer term, the policy of making the regime more vulnerable, something that is an objective of sanctions, and actually pursuing regime change, something that is not, are easily confused and, under certain conditions, nearly indistinguishable. This might increase the value of nuclear weapons to the regime. Although Iran would still face serious obstacles to breaking out, including the near certainty that it would be detected, it might nonetheless take this risk if it were desperate – in turn precipitating a war that would only delay and push the Iranian programme underground. The precedent of Iraq, which was contained at increasing cost for twelve years after the 1991 Gulf War, is a troubling one.

If Iran were to acquire a nuclear weapon, this would have major implications for regional security. Nuclear weapons would preclude forcible regime change through invasion or large-scale intervention, and would inhibit Iran's adversaries from threatening its core territory. However, Iran would struggle to use nuclear weapons for much more than this. Iran could, like Pakistan, increase its assistance to militants safe in the knowledge that retaliation would be limited. However, as explained in Chapter IV, Iran does not enjoy many of the advantages from which Pakistan benefits, and would still be vulnerable to a wide range of conventional military responses from a coalition of far more powerful states. For example, Israel would not be greatly inhibited from, say, striking at Iranian targets or allies in Lebanon, because Iranian nuclear weapons could not credibly protect such assets. Furthermore, it is likely that the US and its allies would have to intensify diplomatic and military support for regional states, which would generate problems of its own at a time when sclerotic Arab regimes have demonstrated their vulnerability to internal political pressures. In Bahrain, for instance, where the US deploys its Fifth Fleet, a series of bombs tore through the capital in November 2012. Two months earlier, the British parliament's Foreign Affairs Committee announced an inquiry into the government's foreign policy towards Saudi Arabia and Bahrain, indicating the sort of domestic political problems that this support can engender.

Turkey, Egypt and Saudi Arabia would be concerned about their traditional rival, Iran, developing nuclear weapons. However, Turkey would enjoy the protection of NATO (including the nuclear weapons based in its territory); Egypt is reassessing its relationship with Iran; and Saudi Arabia – by far the most credible proliferation candidate – would have to consider whether procuring its own nuclear weapons from Pakistan would be worth the risk such an act would pose to the Saudi-American relationship, itself vital to Saudi Arabian security.

The arguments in Chapter IV therefore suggest that proliferation pessimism, the notion that a nuclear Iran would set in motion an unstoppable regional cascade, is somewhat overblown. However, the Middle East has seen a resurgent interest in nuclear power. Iranian nuclear weapons would accelerate that trend, and even states that would not actually pursue nuclear weapons might place greater emphasis on gradually developing a nuclear infrastructure as a hedging option.

The Iranian nuclear crisis has now lasted for over a decade. It was in August 2002 that Iranian exiles, on the basis of leaked American intelligence to the IAEA, announced that Iran had secretly built an enrichment facility and heavy-water reactor. Traditionally, states have been able to build nuclear weapons on far shorter timelines: for instance, the US took just under three years; the Soviet Union four years; the UK six years; France eight years; and China nine years.[2]

During this period, Iran has faced unprecedented coercion, sabotage, interference and scrutiny. This contributed to its decision to pause most of its nuclear-weapons-related research in 2003, and to return to nuclear talks in 2012. However, Iran has shown great determination to preserve a nuclear-enrichment capability even despite these enormous pressures. Its reasons for doing so include, among others, scientific nationalism and prestige, and a desire to keep open the option of producing nuclear weapons in the future. Unless a deal can be reached whereby Iran preserves some of its nuclear infrastructure under conditions that assuage Western concerns, then there is a risk that this decade-old 'permanent crisis' will continue to simmer for many years to come.

[2] Verghese Koithara, *Managing India's Nuclear Forces* (Washington, DC: Brookings Institution, 2012) p. 96.

About Whitehall Papers

The *Whitehall Paper* series provides in-depth studies of specific developments, issues or themes in the field of national and international defence and security. Published occasionally throughout the year, *Whitehall Papers* reflect the highest standards of original research and analysis, and are invaluable background material for specialists and policy-makers alike.

About RUSI

The Royal United Services Institute (RUSI) is an independent think tank engaged in cutting-edge defence and security research. A unique institution, founded in 1831 by the Duke of Wellington, RUSI embodies nearly two centuries of forward thinking, free discussion and careful reflection on defence and security matters.

RUSI consistently brings to the fore vital policy issues to both domestic and global audiences, enhancing its growing reputation as a 'thought-leader institute', winning the Prospect Magazine Think Tank of the Year Award 2008 and Foreign Policy Think Tank of the Year Award 2009 and 2011. RUSI is a British institution, but operates with an international perspective. Satellite offices in Doha and Washington, DC reinforce its global reach. It has amassed over the years an outstanding reputation for quality and objectivity. Its heritage and location at the heart of Whitehall, together with a range of contacts both inside and outside government, give RUSI a unique insight and authority.